ISBN 978-1-0980-4418-3 (paperback)
ISBN 978-1-0980-4520-3 (hardcover)
ISBN 978-1-0980-4419-0 (digital)

Copyright © 2020 by Laura A. Franklin

All rights reserved. No part of this publication may be reproduced, distributed, or transmitted in any form or by any means, including photocopying, recording, or other electronic or mechanical methods without the prior written permission of the publisher. For permission requests, solicit the publisher via the address below.

Christian Faith Publishing, Inc.
832 Park Avenue
Meadville, PA 16335
www.christianfaithpublishing.com

Printed in the United States of America

CONTENTS

Acknowledgments 5
Prelude 7
A Little History 11
Chapter 1: Undershirts 13
Chapter 2: Training Bras 16
Chapter 3: Sports Bras: Change 24
Chapter 4: Wonderbras 44
Chapter 5: Filler Bras: I Want My Mommy! 51
              Words of Encouragement 60
Chapter 6: Angels in My Pocket: Beauty Isn't Seen, It's Shown ... 61
              A Photo Gallery of My Journey and Dedications 65
Chapter 7: My "D" Cup and Me: Grace is a Divine Gratuity 78
Chapter 8: Cross-Your-Heart Bra 86
Chapter 9: Padded Bras 91
Chapter 10: Strapless Bras 98
Chapter 11: Cut and Paste: My Ninth-Hour Experience ... 104
Chapter 12: Bra-Stuffing 101 127
Chapter 13: Underwire Bras 135
Chapter 14: Longline: Push-Up Bras 141
Chapter 15: Final Thoughts 146
Questions for Reflection/Journaling/Notes 151

ACKNOWLEDGMENTS

First and foremost, I would like to thank my Lord and Savior, Jesus Christ, for His leading, comfort, and healing while trekking this journey. Nothing gets to me without His permission. I was chosen to walk this road not once but twice. By His stripes, I am healed.

To my momma, Eloise Johnson, you fought cancer like a champ. Not once but twice. It is because of your modeling, mentoring, and having the demeanor that is reverential that I was able to stay strong. Words cannot express how your faith, your sober thinking, your love for your family, and your sacrifice has made me who I am today. Because of you, I can! To the many male and female Washington family members who were diagnosed with lung, brain, breast, throat, and prostate cancer and God decided to call you home early, I love and thank you. To my eight older siblings, I praise God it was none of you. It is my prayer that this disease will end with me and not pass on to the next generation.

To my big sister Liz. Thank you for leaving the comforts of your home to come take care of me when I couldn't take care of myself. I love you.

To my godchildren. Thank you for being there for me, sitting with me until I fell asleep, rubbing my feet, buying me foods I wasn't supposed to have—wink, wink—and to all my adopted godchildren, nieces, and nephews, Auntie loves and appreciates you.

To my church family, thank you for your prayers, visits, cards, gifts, and for loving me and my family through this journey. To Pastors M, G, and L, thank you for being you.

To my little sister, thank you is not nearly enough for what you've done for me. Sigh.

To Ricky Jones, thank you for being such a great childhood friend and loving me as I was. I can still see your smiling face. Rest in heaven, my dear friend.

To those women who feel they are not whole, I tell you that you are! Stories of tragedy and triumph are never easy to write, even if you've come out on top. It requires you to relive each moment as if it just happened. The smells, sounds, pictures, people, and experiences are fresh and very real. I found myself laughing and crying often while writing, remembering the hurt, mean words, true love, and the struggles of life. Cancer does not give you the option to be private. Nor does it play favorites. It does not care what your name is, how much money you have, where you grew up, who your parents are, or what you believe in. Its only purpose is to shake your foundation, distract your attention from your faith, make you feel helpless, and perhaps claim your life.

Lastly, to my children, Jonathan, Jedidiah Sr., Deion, Derick, and Mara, thank you for *literally* walking with me through the diagnosis and healing. Each of you walked behind me, up and down the stairs, to be sure I didn't fall; for keeping track of my uh-ohs on a regular basis, pulling up my pants when I sagged, and praying for me while I was ill. To my grandchildren, Jedidiah Abram B. Washington Jr. and Zoe Michelle Washington, you are the new joys of my life and La-La loves you more than I understand. Keep your dukes up.

These stories are true to life. Some names have been changed or omitted to protect privacy. Bra-stuffers—*unite*!

PRELUDE

Since I can remember, someone has been praying for me. Some were asked to and some were not. I had a rocky start as an infant. I was left in the hospital after I was born because my mother took the wrong baby. As my mother reached the exit of the hospital, the charge nurse shouted to her, "You have the wrong baby!" There were two babies born on the same day. Both black girls and both had the last name of Washington. Man, I could've been with a rich family. I was sickly as a toddler with scarlet fever. It was relentless and would not be broken. My grandmother and mother didn't know what else to do for me except to pray. The doctors didn't know what to do for me either. I was sent back home and my family was told to keep me comfortable.

One day, while I was still dealing with the fever, an unknown male stopped by the house and spoke to my grandmother. My grandmother was careful not to let him in the house.

"You have a sick baby in the house and I need to pray for her," he said. My grandmother was a God-fearing woman but she was also particular about folks.

"You can pray for her on the porch," she replied. The man prayed for me through the door. Miraculously the next day, I was fine.

I have had scarlet fever three times in my lifetime. The first time was the time I just mentioned. The next time was when I was six or seven years old. And the third time was when I was twenty-five years old. Scarlet fever is not a glamorous illness. Many have died from it, especially children. But God had a plan for me.

I remember, during my second challenge with this fever, my mother putting me in a cool tub repeatedly in attempts to bring my fever down. I also remember hearing her, crying out to the Lord about it. She held me in her arms, rocked me, and prayed. I could also hear her moaning in a way of deep pain and hurt. At the time, I didn't know she was mourning over me, but now, I know that is what she was doing. She didn't know anything else to do but give me over to God. The prayers obviously worked because the next thing I remember was running outside to play with my siblings.

The third time I had scarlet fever was in 1992. Doctors had given me up for dead once again. I had broken out in hives all over my body, had a fever of 104.8, and I had to be quarantined until my fever cleared or until I died. The doctors stuck me in a room the size of a hospital storage closet. I had a television, a toilet, but I didn't have a phone. This same year, I was struggling with so many issues. I was a single mother of two toddlers, ages three and two years old. I was having a hard time paying my rent and utility bills on time due to being sick and in the hospital for so long. And to make matters worse, my landlord thought I skipped town and he broke into my apartment, stole some of my electronics as compensation, and changed the locks on the door. I recalled my hospital experience often, wondering what else God was doing. Because the doctors and nurses had given me up for dead, I decided to give myself up to God. I surrendered my life to God's will that night, and if he decided to take me, I was ready. I straightened my linen around me so if the Lord took me that night, the bed would be neat. I placed my hands at my side, closed my eyes, and surrendered. The next morning, my fever was broken. All of my clothing, including my bedding, was soaked. Somebody was praying! God had a plan for me.

As it is with so many of us, I experienced childhood trauma. I was sexually offended by a few male family friends. My biological father and I had a nonexistent relationship, and in high school, I was in a physical, mental, and verbally abusive relationship at the age of sixteen. During this time, I felt like I had no one to tell. I knew to pray for myself. However, I didn't know how to go to the Word for strength, but God had a plan for me.

I STUFF MY BRA... *SO WHAT?*

I have experienced a lot. My big sister and best friend Dee-Dee was murdered on December 18, 1987. My maternal grandmother, with whom I was extremely close, died in January 2001. She was my prayer warrior. She taught me to pray by teaching me the Lord's Prayer and then moving on to petitioning in my prayers. I used to sit outside my grandmother's bedroom door and listen to her read Scriptures then pray when she was done. There were a few times she allowed me in the room to kneel with her, read the Bible, and pray.

My mother was diagnosed with breast cancer in 1990. I was so afraid I would lose her that I backed away. Thinking I would have to raise my boys without her was more than I could take. I cried often when she wasn't around so she couldn't see my tears. I didn't attend any of her appointments with her because, in my mind, cancer equated death. Due to the cancer spreading to her lymph nodes, she was encouraged to have a mastectomy. When I saw her in the hospital recovery room, I cried and wouldn't go in any further to see her. Through all of her chemotherapy treatments and doctor's visits in between, she smiled and never complained.

In March of 1997, my mother married a wonderful man named Robert Taylor Johnson. At their reception, Robert spoke to the crowd.

"Eloise's family is now my family, her children and grandchildren are my children and grandchildren and all I have is yours."

From that day forward, he was my dad. I called him Dad or Daddy. My other siblings called him Robert or Papa Robert.

In August 2001, I was diagnosed with DCIS (ductal carcinoma in situ) breast cancer. In May 2005, I was the first in my family to earn a college degree. In November 2006, when I thought I was done with this disease, more calcium clusters were found in another part of the same breast. In May 2010, I earned my bachelor's degree. Through being involved in different ministries at church, marriage, school and homework, five children, radiation treatments, multiple small bouts of depression because of the cancer, life changes, and the loss of my grandmother and mother, God was there and He had a plan for my life.

This book was written to share the journey where, in the end, I win because of God. I am not trying to be famous, just effective. It is my hope that you will read this book and be encouraged to fight this disease and remember the survivors in your life—those who continue to fight presently—and cheer them on with your prayers, kind words, and honest visits.

A LITTLE HISTORY

A woman stuffing her bra has occurred since the bra was invented. Women who performed on stage, actresses, grandmothers, mothers, athletes, women in the workplace, and even church ladies have stuffed their bras. Only back then, it was called wearing "falsies." And now it's called enhancing womanhood. Nonetheless, it happened. I used to watch my cousins, aunts, and some of my older sisters' friends put falsies in their bras. It didn't make sense to me why they needed or wanted extra when they should have been happy with what they had. But that was before my journey with bra stuffing began and I had anything to contend with. And now, my story.

UNDERSHIRTS

It provides insulation when needed and some are worn to "compress" the figure in a slimming attempt. But for the most part, it's a barrier for sweat and to prevent the viewing of what's underneath.

I was nine years old when I first tried stuffing my bra. My sister Dee-Dee, who was nineteen months older than me, blossomed like she had special breast soil fed to her every night. It seemed like each day, her chest flourished with joy. And she smiled at them like they were freshly fried pieces of chicken on a Sunday after church. Teenage boys and grown men alike stared at them. To me, she was already a woman and I wanted to be one too.

I had always been a late bloomer, especially in the chest-developing department, so I had to be covert with my operation. Because I hadn't developed yet, I had to wear undershirts. I thought undershirts were for babies or small children to wear during the winter when it was cold. Undershirts were for little girls. Undershirts were for old men over thirty who smoked. Undershirts were not for a blossoming young lady such as myself. So to fit in with the big girls,

I hatched a plan. I decided to get up super early to prepare. I took my bath the night before so all I had to do was get to the bathroom first. As I took out my stash of toilet paper, I hid behind the towels on the shelf; I was shaking with excitement and fear. I had to hurry before everyone woke up and I had to make sure it was done right. I balled up, wrapped up, and folded the toilet paper over and over again. As I heard footsteps approaching the bathroom door, I got scared and accidentally dropped the remainder of the roll in the toilet. Good thing there wasn't anything in there. I threw away the wet roll and quickly exited the bathroom. I kept my chest covered with a towel, as if I had just taken a bath, so no one would see my creations. It was time to leave for school. I purposely took my time so I could walk by myself. I carried my books in front of me so no one would notice. It was a nice spring day so I couldn't hide behind my jacket. As I walked to school, I made sure to stay behind my sister Dee-Dee and her friends so they couldn't see me.

My big brother Vincent ran up behind me and asked me why I had a tail. I looked at him in confusion. As he pointed to my issue, I realized I had left a long trail of toilet paper hanging out of the back of my shirt. Pretending I didn't know where it was coming from, I tried to play it off and laughed but my big brother wouldn't let it go. He kept saying how stupid I looked. I yelled to him to leave me alone but he wouldn't. By this time, we had caught up to my sister and her friends. She yelled at him as well to stop teasing me but he was relentless. In my embarrassment and error, I took my books away from my chest—and there they were for everyone to see. I had two massive bulky toilet-paper breasts. If I thought I was humiliated before, this was the thing that sent me over the top. The entire group, including my sister, burst out laughing. I was frozen! I just cried and ran back home. When I got there, my mom was still getting ready for work. She asked me why I was back and I couldn't say a word through my tears. Eventually I had to show and tell her, and she just smiled at me. That made me feel worse because her look confirmed I was still a little girl. My mother told me to get changed and come into my room.

See, no one told me how much to put in my bra or how to stuff it. Having breasts seemed like it was such a big deal to other women and young girls and I wanted to be and look like them. I didn't know there was an art form to stuffing my bra. I just wanted to be loved, accepted, and to be a woman.

"Laura, having breasts, large or small, don't make you a woman. It's what God put inside of you that makes you a woman."

"You can say that because you have them already," I told her.

She then hugged me so tight I almost burst.

"Can I stay home from school?" I asked.

"You can't run away from your problems," she said. "I'll take care of your brother and sister later," she assured me. She made me go to school, even though I was late.

Although my mom made me feel better at the time, all of that was shattered when I got to school. The rumor had spread about my bulky paper breasts. Needless to say, that was the worst day I ever experienced in school up to that point. Through my tears and shame, I still held my head high and smiled inside because of what my mom told me and knowing the satisfaction I would have later when my older siblings got home from school. That night, I vowed never to stuff my bra again. But God had another plan.

TRAINING BRAS

It's supposed to train the breast. It does not train the breasts but provides protection and support for developing buds.

As a young girl, I was sheltered from certain things in life. Growing up Southern and Baptist kept me out of *some* trouble; but the older I got, the less Baptist I acted as a way of rebelling. Having a praying grandmother, mother, aunts, and neighbors steered me back on course. God had to know I was going to deal with all of the ridiculous issues a child like me would have. I am the youngest of nine children and, might I add, the cutest and smartest. Most people would think growing up the youngest and being a girl meant I got what I wanted. Not so. In fact, it was the complete opposite. I do thank God Almighty that by the time my mother got to whippin' my behind that she was too tired because of the eight siblings that came before me. We lovingly called our mother Madea. I think she whipped me five times in my lifetime. With one of them, she tried to kill me. That's because I told her I wished I was dead so I didn't have to clean the kitchen. She failed in granting my wish and I still had to clean the kitchen. As I grew up, I learned from my older brothers and sisters what to do and what not to do. My sister Dee-Dee, God rest her soul, never learned that. Her mouth got her into trouble more times than I could count. Nonetheless, though I didn't know at the time, all of this was preparation for what life would hand me and how God would deliver me over and over again.

When I was nine years old, my grandmother made me wear a training bra. I didn't understand why since there wasn't anything to "train." *Is there a true purpose for wearing this thing*? I thought to myself. Of course, there was no answer for me; so reluctantly, I wore it. The women in my life at that time all wore a *real* bra. I wanted to wear one too. But I was so flat that when my *loving* brothers and their friends spoke to me, they called me names like ironing board, surfboard, and a sidewalk. I'd stick my tongue at them and twist my face. It hurt to hear those words but what could I do? My sister Dee-Dee began to develop as a young woman at the age of nine. It was like she drank breast fertilizer. I thought boys liked her for her brains and winning smile, but later, I found out that they never asked her questions and their eyes rarely stared at her face.

The training bras I wore were handed down from my cousins so they were already trained, but I was obedient and wore them. They had little butterflies in the center of them and were very uncomfortable because they slid around all the time, mostly upward. I had to wear them each day when I went to school and I was so embarrassed. On my first day of training—a Friday—the boys in Alabama noticed when my wardrobe changed. This was because most of the time, I wore white tops. I might as well have been wearing a neon sign over my head that said, "Look at me. I'm wearing a training bra!" I was so afraid to wear that darn thing. The boys either laughed at me or let the entire fifth-grade class know I had one on. The girls made ugly faces at me. Thank God for a Christian teacher, Mrs. Garey. After watching the kids point and laugh at me on the blacktop, she walked over to me, wrapped her arm around me.

"Honey, they're just jealous because God's got something special for you!" she said.

"Thank you," I said. "But do you think He could give it to me now?"

My teacher just grinned and walked back to the classroom. I was impatient as a child. I couldn't wait for God to show up with His "special" gift. On the way home, I started letting my mind wander on how I could show the kids on the playground just how special I was.

Over the weekend, I made up a plan on how I would get back at the kids at school. Even in Sunday school, I got into trouble because I was daydreaming about my revenge. After church, we went straight home. I prayed and prayed that God would make this work. I couldn't wait to go to bed. I ate my dinner quickly, and I only watched an hour of television. I took my bath, said my prayers—a really good one for the next school day—then went to sleep. I imagined how things would go and how stupid those kids would look when they saw me. I was up before the alarm clock went off (before my mom came in, that is). I ran into the bathroom to get ready for school. I used the back bathroom for privacy. My older siblings kept yelling for me to hurry up so we wouldn't be late.

"I'm coming!" I said.

I hurried out of the bathroom, grabbed my books, and ran out the door. I didn't even kiss my mom goodbye. While my siblings and I walked to school, I thought about the kids' reaction to seeing me. A voice broke up my thoughts.

"Hey," the voice said.

It was Ricky Jones from down the street. Ricky had a crush on me from the first day of fifth grade and he was not shy about it. To me, he was bothersome and smelled funny. We let him walk with us anyway. All he talked about was how he and I would get married someday and have three kids. He hoped the girls would look like me and the boys looked like him. I hoped he would get hit by a car. While Ricky continued his verbal fantasy, I let my thoughts carry me to the playground and his voice faded.

As we approached our school, my older brothers and sister told me to be careful and have a good day. Ricky and I parted from the group and they walked on to the junior high school.

"Can I carry your books?" Ricky asked.

"No, thank you. I'm fine," I replied defiantly.

I STUFF MY BRA... *SO WHAT?*

I knew that if I let him carry my books, that would mean something to the other kids and I didn't want them thinking he was my boyfriend. I could see the kids playing tetherball on the far side of the blacktop. Ricky and I walked over to them and asked if we could play next.

"Are you sure your bra won't fall down when you swing, Laura?" one of the girls asked.

All of the kids laughed.

"Shut up and leave her alone!" Ricky said in my defense.

"That's okay," I said. I turned around, put my books down, unzipped my jacket and turned around to face the group. All I could hear was a resounding gasp.

"Are we gonna play tetherball or what?" I asked.

"Laura, look down!" Ricky said, pointing to my chest.

I looked down and saw that I had smashed my newly developed breasts. Again I stuffed my bra with toilet paper, hoping this time, it would work. No one told me that I couldn't wear a sweater over them or that I shouldn't carry my books too close to my chest because they would die. Next thing I knew, everyone on God's green earth was laughing at me. It was so loud that I didn't hear the bell ring to signify school had started. To add to my humiliation, they were lopsided too. The training bra I wore had slid up over the toilet paper and smashed my left fake breast in half. Ricky tried to stop them from teasing me but his efforts failed.

The teacher yelled to us, saying to come inside. The laughing group went inside first while I lagged behind.

"Hurry up, Laura," my teacher yelled.

When I looked up at her, she saw that I was crying.

"What's wrong?" she asked.

I showed her my creation. She told me to go to the office to get cleaned up. Ricky volunteered to walk me to the office and the teacher agreed. We walked in silence for what seemed like ten miles. Before I walked into the office, Ricky, with his smelly body and odd-shaped face, said, "I'm sorry. I love you just the way you are."

I walked into the office and never looked back at him to say thanks. I was too ashamed to tell the nurse what really happened so

I told her I threw up on the playground. She called my mother, and I went to the bathroom before she showed up, threw my breasts in the trash, and sat down in the waiting room and prayed she wouldn't find out the truth. *I'd failed again*, I thought to myself. I was so frustrated with my body.

"Do you want some crackers when you get home?" Madea asked.

"Yes, ma'am," I replied.

"You can sleep in my bed if you want to," Madea said.

"Thank you." Sleeping in her bed always made the bad things go away.

While I ate my soup and crackers in my mom's bed, I replayed the horror of my day over and over in my mind. But what I remember most was Ricky trying to defend me. I closed my eyes and prayed that God would take me to heaven in my sleep so the kids would feel bad for teasing me. That didn't happen because when I opened my eyes again, only two hours had gone by.

"Get up and go wash your face, then come to the kitchen," Madea told me.

I did as I was told and she had something waiting for me on the table. It was the most glorious piece of homemade pound cake with vanilla ice cream on top. My favorite! I ate as if it was my last meal. Madea found out what happened at school because Ricky called the house to check on me. He filled her in on all the gory details.

"How was it?" Madea asked, referring to the cake and ice cream.

"Delicious!" I said.

She left the room and came back with a paper bag. She sat it on the table and told me to open it. My eyes grew to the size of saucers when I looked inside. The bag was full of toilet paper. I forgot to put away what I didn't use this morning before I went to school. My mother found it while she was cleaning up. All of a sudden, that cake and ice cream didn't taste so good. Had I known she knew, I would have made that food last till midnight.

After I ate my cake and ice cream, my mother took me back into her room and whipped my behind. I tried to grab the bag of tissue to stuff my pants but she snatched me back like I was attached

I STUFF MY BRA... SO WHAT?

to a rubber band on her arm. She told me she whipped me for lying. Had I told the truth, I wouldn't have been punished.

"Train up a child in the way he should go. When he is old he will not depart from it," Grandmother said as she passed by. "That was from the book of Proverbs in the Bible."

I went to my room and cried myself to sleep. I was supposed to take a bath but my behind was too sore. My sister Dee-Dee woke me up in the middle of the night.

"What happened?" she asked.

"I didn't tell Madea the truth," I said.

Even in the dark, she could tell by the tone of my voice that I didn't want to talk about it. She rolled over toward me, hugged me, and we fell asleep together. That night, I was glad to have a big sister.

When I saw Ricky at school the next day, I socked him and kept walking. When we got into the classroom, it was as if they had forgotten about what happened to me the day before. No one was laughing or pointing at me. I later found out that our teacher told them if they teased me about the incident that their parents would be called. Back then, calling mommas from their jobs was deadly to black children in the South.

Ricky sat behind me in class. He kept pulling my ponytails from the back. *Stupid boy*, I thought. *Just wait until recess*. When the bell rang for recess, I was the first one out the door so I could get a red ball and smash it in Ricky's face for pulling my hair. But before I could do that, he handed me a note. It had hearts and flowers on it. When I opened it up, it read, "Do you like me yes or no?" I frowned at first, but then I thought about it. On our way home, we talked about what only fifth graders talk about, school of course. A small moment of silence passed, then he spoke.

"Did you read the note?"

"Yes," I said.

That was all he got out of me for the rest of our walk home. We arrived at my house and went our separate ways. I turned back and handed Ricky his note back. As he opened it, his eyes grew wide as if he'd won the lottery. I circled "yes" on the note.

"Thanks, Laura!" he said.

He smiled at me and ran all the way home. I walked up the stairs to the front door, and as I walked inside, I had a big grin on my face. My grandmother was in the front room and saw the exchange between me and Ricky.

"Laura Ann, that boy is nasty and he needs a bath," Grandmother said.

I thought to myself, *She's right*. I went to my room, did my homework, and wrote his name on everything I owned. Yes, he was weird, smelled bad, and had a funny-shaped head, but he liked me for me and that was all that mattered.

Time passed and before I knew it, Ricky and I had been boyfriend and girlfriend for three months now. That's like a year for a fifth grader.

"Can I kiss you?" he asked.

"No! I'm a good girl!" I replied. Plus, my granny and momma would tear my tail up." There were four things I did not do as a Southern Baptist child. I did not wear red stockings to church. I did not wear pants to church. I did not chew gum in church. And I certainly did not kiss a boy without permission. I knew I wasn't going to get permission so about a week later, my brother Vincent and I pretended to go to the park to meet friends but we were really going so I could see Ricky.

Vincent was my lookout for adults, teenagers, and mostly Madea. Ricky and I sat on the picnic table at The Old Man Park. We called it that because only old men would sit at the park during the day because they were bored at home. They played cards and checkers every day. But mostly they argued about politics, their wives, and money. While we sat at the table, swinging our feet, we kept looking around to see who was looking. We were both afraid of getting caught together and for kissing. Today was strange because Ricky didn't smell funny. His hair was combed and his head seemed to have rounded out some.

"Hurry up, fools!" my brother Vincent shouted!

So we did. We kissed. I think it lasted all of ten seconds, maybe more. I didn't really know. Nor did I care. I had gotten my first kiss at The Old Man Park! I gave Ricky the ribbon from my hair and ran off to meet up with my brother. I ran as fast as I could. I smiled all the way home. I was a woman now! That day, I learned that true friends are there, no matter what. And smelly boys, if they just take a bath, can be your boyfriend. Ricky loved me for me and that was more important than anything in the world. Well, that and not getting caught.

SPORTS BRAS: CHANGE

*This bra restrains the breasts so that they
don't move too much during activity.
They help maintain the integrity of
the breast wall and its shape.*

Growing up the youngest of nine children and having five brothers was exciting! Everything my big brothers did, I did. Every sport they played, I played. Madea tried her best to keep me in frilly dresses and socks with lace on them but it didn't work. I would leave the house looking like I was on my way to Sunday brunch, and when I returned, I looked like I had been a part of Sunday's football game.

"Eloise, I don't know why you put that yellow dress on her. You know it will come back green," Granny stated.

"I'm tryin', Momma," Madea replied.

My mother would just shake her head. I didn't get it either. In junior high, I ran track, was on the basketball team, and played coed flag football. Football was my favorite sport. I played quarterback and wide receiver. I had a powerful arm, fast legs, and good hands for catching the ball. Most boys were either afraid of me or picked on me.

I STUFF MY BRA... *SO WHAT?*

With junior high came all the challenges of elementary school to the power of ten. The same kids that laughed at me in fifth grade had not forgotten about the bra-stuffing incident. They chose to remind me every chance they got. But because I was more mature now, I would beat up the boys and threaten the girls. My future in junior high was secure.

Ricky and I had been boyfriend and girlfriend off and on now for a year. He showered regularly and got taller. Somehow he wasn't as cute as he was when he was ten. He still carried my books for me and walked me home every day and he kissed me at the corner before I got to my door so my granny and Madea wouldn't see. But who did see us, every day, was Mrs. Nelson. She was my granny's next-door neighbor, church lady, and very good friend. She was the sweetest lady in the world. The day I found out she knew about Ricky and me, she called me to her front porch. It was screened in to keep the flies out.

"Uh-huh. That boy gon' get you in trouble one day," she said.

I was startled and looked up.

"Hi, Mrs. Nelson. How ya doin'?"

"Not as good as you," she replied with a sinister laugh.

I twisted my face at her and walked to her porch.

"Are you gonna tell on me?"

"I won't tell," she said. "You shouldn't sneak around kissing boys."

"It was just one boy, Mrs. Nelson," I responded.

Mrs. Nelson always had fresh lemonade on her porch. I stared at it, licking my lips.

"Can I have some lemonade?"

"Not until you wipe your lips. I don't want boy germs on my drinking glasses," she replied.

We both laughed but she was serious. I wiped my face with the towel she handed to me and drank the lemonade from a brown-tinted glass. We sat and talked for about an hour. Though two years had passed since I first began wearing bras, mine still wasn't quite filled. As I looked down at my shirt, Mrs. Nelson saw that I was concerned about something.

"What's wrong, Laura?" she asked.

"My bras won't fill up, Mrs. Nelson. Why?"

"It takes time, dear. Be patient."

"Patience is something I don't have. It seems as if every girl in junior high had something in their bras except me. Other sixth graders have something to show but not me," I said, whining.

"God saves His best for last," Mrs. Nelson said.

I rolled my eyes away from Mrs. Nelson.

"You know, Laura, there's these things called falsies. Women put them in their bras to fill 'em up."

"Really?"

"Yes!" she said. "I'm sure your mother has some, your grandmother too. In fact, I know your grandmother does. We were lookin' at 'em in the store last week."

"Thank you, Mrs. Nelson!"

I ran to the house. Mrs. Nelson didn't realize the idea she had given me. My mind began to race with so many options. I had to get my shower before going to the dinner table. Granny didn't think young ladies should smell like yardbirds during dinner. While I was in the tub, I prayed to God that this next idea would work.

Mrs. Nelson and I talked daily on her porch after school and on the weekends. We talked about boys and music. She taught me how to sew a button on my shirt and how to make figs into something to eat as a sandwich spread. I didn't eat 'em but I enjoyed spending time with her. Her house was crowded with furniture. She also had a small organ to play music on. She'd let me play it once in a while. Or until my granny called me back to the house. Meanwhile I was making plans.

"Our day is coming, guys! Just hold on!" I said to my slowly developing breasts.

I went into the bathroom after dinner. I was looking into the mirror at my chest. I was deep in thought when I heard someone bang on the door.

"Hurry up! Them thangs ain't gon' grow no more!"

It was my brother Vincent. Out of all my siblings, he was the closest to me, but he could also be one of the meanest to me. I turned

I STUFF MY BRA… *SO WHAT?*

to the side to see if there was any change in my chest. There wasn't. I twisted my face up at myself in the mirror, turned off the light, and walked out. I went into the kitchen and took two tangerines off the table. I went into my room. When I lay in bed, I thought to myself, *Surely God knows how bad I want them to grow, right?* I placed the tangerines in my shirt with the hopes that one day, they would grow to that size. I then rolled over on my side and the tangerines rolled out from under my shirt. I shook my head, threw them on the chair by the bed, and went to sleep. I didn't even pray. I was so discouraged.

Easter break was fast approaching and I couldn't wait to be away from school and away from the drama and the reminders of my lack of development. I had plans to play stickball in the street with my brothers and cousins every morning and climb the pecan tree behind the house. Ricky and I walked home from school, and as we approached my house, I ran ahead of him to see my mom before she left for work.

"Hey! What about my kiss?" he shouted!

I shooed him away and kept running. Just as my mom was pulling out of the driveway, she told me to make sure I did all my homework because when she got home, we were going to have a family meeting.

"Yes, ma'am!" I replied.

I just knew we were going to Atlanta for our Easter break. I made sure my homework and chores were done before Madea got home. We sat around the table, waiting to hear the good news. When she entered the room, she had a sad look on her face. All of us knew the news wasn't good.

"We're moving!" she said through a deep breath.

"*What!*" Dee-Dee shouted.

"*Where!*" Vincent asked.

"*When!*" I asked.

"Hold on!" Madea said. "We are moving to Atlanta and we're moving while you're on Easter break."

You would have thought Jesus came back and didn't take us with Him with all the loud screams we let out. My sister Dee-Dee was the only one glad for the move. My brothers were not happy because they had so many friends. I wasn't happy because I had to leave Ricky. But I was glad to leave those who made it their life's work to tease me each day.

"Make sure you say your goodbyes to everyone in the next two weeks," Madea said.

I couldn't wait to call Ricky and tell him what was going on. We cried on the phone for Lord knows how long. Then my granny picked up the other line to listen to our conversation.

"I gotta go, Ricky," I said in a sad voice and quickly hung up the phone and went to talk to my sister Dee-Dee.

Dee-Dee was so excited about moving to the big city of Atlanta that she started packing the same night. I went to bed early. I was glad about leaving this place so I wouldn't have to deal with the smell anymore. We didn't live far from the paper mill and every day, all day, the stench of the paper was like smelling sewage. I thought of leaving my boyfriend and my friends. I no longer felt special to God. I felt He had left me hanging. Didn't He care that I would be sad?

The next two weeks was full of thoughts that clouded my mind about a new house, new friends, new schools, new everything. I didn't accept change well. While helping out in the kitchen, I had a side conversation with my mom.

"Madea, where will we live in Atlanta?" I asked.

"We will share a home with your uncle and aunt until I can find something for all of us," she responded.

"Why do we have to leave?" I asked.

"It's what's best for us right now," Madea said.

Years later, I found out we moved because my biological father wanted us closer to him and my granny didn't like him and he wasn't allowed in her home. During the next couple of weeks, before spring break, Ricky and I spent as much time together as we possibly could. We spent most of our time at The Old Man Park, kissing. That's all we knew how to do. I was hoping my shirt would fill out before we left so I'd have something to show in the new city. That was asking for too much from God though, I thought.

"Don't find a new boyfriend while you're away from me," Ricky requested.

I STUFF MY BRA… *SO WHAT?*

"I won't. All them boys are probably ugly anyway," I replied. But then I thought to myself, *Ricky was ugly too when I met him but look at him now.*

"Make sure you stay in touch too. I want you to call me all the time," Ricky said.

"I will. I promise," I said.

Ricky gave me his address and his grandmother's address. Back then, grandparents and parents didn't move so I was sure to find him whenever I wanted.

Moving day was the next day. Dee-Dee was sent ahead with three of my other brothers. She was helping my aunt and uncle with babysitting. Madea packed my things because I didn't know what I was doing. My brother Vincent was all packed and ready to go.

"I'll bake y'all a cake and fry some chicken and put a loaf of white bread in the basket for the road," Granny said. My mother decided to drive since it was only five hours to Atlanta.

While packing the car with our belongings, the next morning, Ricky stopped by.

"Good morning, Mrs. Washington," he said to my mother.

"Good morning, son."

"May I speak with Laura before you leave?" he asked.

"Yes. That's fine," she replied.

Ricky and I walked to the backyard for privacy. He handed me a black box.

"What's in it?" I asked.

"Just open it," he said.

When I opened the box, there was a picture of him from the fifth grade and a current picture of him from school.

"What's this for?" I asked.

"So you'll remember how it was when we met and how you've changed my life since."

This boy was deep, I thought to myself.

"Okay. Thanks," I replied.

"Look under the pictures," he insisted.

When I removed the pictures of Ricky, I saw he had given me a key glued to a heart. He saw the strange look on my face.

"I'm giving you the key to my heart. Don't lose it," he said.

Ricky began to cry and it was about all I could take, standing there, watching him.

"Quit your whining!" I said. "I'll be back to visit my grandmother and we can see each other then."

Deep down, I wanted to cry too; but the tomboy in me wouldn't allow it. I too gave Ricky a gift. Mine was in a much larger box than his.

"What's inside?" he asked.

"Open it and see!" I replied with excitement.

When Ricky opened the box, his eyes grew wide.

"What is this?" he asked.

"It's my first bra. The one I wore in fifth grade," I said.

"Why is there so much tissue in this box?" he asked.

"I wanted you to know how special you made me feel the day you defended me in front of all the kids on the blacktop. I will never forget that day. You loved me how I was and that made all the difference in the world to me." I could no longer hold back my tears. We both hugged and cried.

"Laura Ann!" Madea shouted in a slave owner's voice.

"Yes, ma'am?" I replied.

"Let that boy go and come on!"

"I love you," Ricky said.

"I love you too!"

"See you later, Mrs. Jones," Ricky shouted.

I smiled and walked away from him, heading toward the car. Mrs. Nelson was on the front porch as we were getting ready to leave.

"Well, I guess I have to keep some lemonade on the porch for when you come back," she stated.

"Thank you, Mrs. Nelson. I will miss you more than any other adult, besides my granny," I said.

"Is that nasty boy gonna follow you to Atlanta?" she asked.

"I hope so. He loves me," I said with a smile on my face.

"So do I," she said.

I ran to her and gave her a very long hug. I drank the last glass of lemonade I would have for a while.

I STUFF MY BRA... SO WHAT?

"Be particular in Atlanta," Mr. Nelson said.

All the time I had known Mrs. Nelson, Mr. Nelson didn't say much to me other than hello and goodbye. Whenever he did have a complete sentence, it was profound. I hugged him too and gave him a kiss on the cheek. I told both of them thank you for being so nice to me and to save me some apple jelly for the next time I come by. They waved to me and Mrs. Nelson wiped her eyes and went inside. I slept most of the way to Atlanta. I didn't even wake up when we stopped for gas. I had cried myself to sleep.

We arrived in the early afternoon to my aunt and uncle's house. It was small from the outside but much bigger once I went inside. The house was right next to the school Dee-Dee and I would attend. Dee-Dee ran out to meet with us and I swear her boobs looked like they'd grown more. I thought for sure God had forgotten about me and my request now two years ago.

"Hey, y'all!" Dee-Dee said loudly.

How did she get so country so quick? I thought to myself. We were from California.

"Grab a bag, Laura Ann!" Madea said.

I went to the back of the car and carried two bags out. Of course, Dee-Dee and her boobs couldn't help us because she was too fragile now. My brother Vincent and I cleared everything out of the car and took the bags to our rooms.

"Welcome to Atlanta!" Dee-Dee shouted!

I wondered why she was talking so loud.

"Welcome to Atlanta!" my aunt and uncle said in harmony.

They were loud too. I guess that was a normal thing in this area. The phone rang and I ran to pick it up.

"Hello?" I said.

"May I speak to Laura?"

"This is Laura."

"It's Ricky!"

I'd forgotten I gave him this number. I was a little upset because he didn't even give me time to get settled.

"Are you there?" he asked.

"Yeah. I'm here." I replied.

"How's Atlanta?" he asked.

"I don't know. I just got here twenty minutes ago," I responded with annoyance in my voice.

"Okay," he said.

I didn't feel like talking to him at the moment so I excused myself.

"Can I call you back later, Ricky?"

"Yeah. What time?" he asked.

"I don't know. Just later."

"Okay. I love you. Bye," he said.

"Bye," I said. Then I hung up.

My brother Vincent and I went outside to explore the neighborhood. There were only a few kids outside in the yard. We walked over to a house where there was a girl and a boy in the front yard. They looked to be about our ages.

"Hey," the girl said.

"Hi," Vincent said.

"What's y'all name?" the boy asked.

"I'm Vincent, and this is my baby sister, Laura."

"Where y'all from?" she asked.

"California," Vincent replied.

"Y'all know any movie stars?" the boy asked.

"No," I responded.

I was slightly annoyed. Everyone we'd met since we'd gotten to the south side had asked us that question.

"What are your names?" I asked.

"This is my brother, Prince, and my name is Princess."

"Those are your birth names?" I asked.

"Yes," Princess replied.

"Okay. Well, I'm going back to the house. See you later," I stated. "You coming?" I asked Vincent.

"You go on, baby sister. I'm going to stay here."

He had found a cute girl who seemed interested in him. Princess's brother went into the house and the two of them were left alone. Later that night, Madea sent Dee-Dee to find my brother and he was at Princess's house, in the living room, on the couch, kissing that girl. Dee-Dee was not surprised. Vincent had talent, and nine times out of ten, he probably sang to her and that's all she needed to be convinced he was the one.

Starting a new school toward the end of the school year was not easy. I was able to make a few friends. One of them lived down the street from us. His name was Otis. Otis was a year older than me and he had an older sister named Tracy. The school we attended hosted grades kindergarten to eighth grade. Vincent, Dee-Dee, and I were in the same school. Otis had a go-kart and he'd give me rides to the store on it once in a while.

"How old are you?" Otis asked.

"Eleven, going on twelve. Why?"

"How old is your sister?"

"Twelve, going on thirteen," I replied.

"Her boobs are awfully big for a thirteen-year-old!" he exclaimed.

"Yup!" I said with irritation. "Can you take me back to the house please? I don't feel good."

"You on your period or something?" he asked.

"You're stupid! And you have a waterhead!" I said to him.

"If I'm stupid, then get outta my go-kart then!"

"Fine! I don't wanna ride in this raggedy thing anyway," I said loudly.

Otis stopped the go-kart and I got off. I didn't realize I still had at least five blocks to walk. These were not five simple blocks. These were five country blocks. I didn't care. He made me mad and hurt my feelings by talking about Dee-Dee and her boobs. I had boobs too, sorta. My chest had grown some but not to where people didn't think I was a boy. Thank God my hair was long enough.

I spoke to Ricky as often as I could but not as often as he wanted. I was busy running around the city being a tomboy. I was playing soccer and football at school. I enjoyed playing football. The boys in the school didn't like it because I had a strong arm for throwing. That year, I learned that if I wanted a boyfriend, I couldn't be better at sports than them. I didn't want a boyfriend. I wanted to beat boys at sports. Though I didn't see him for a while, Ricky was all I could handle right now.

The next couple years would prove that nature and boys are cruel. My bumps on my chest got a little bigger but not big enough for me. If I could do a comparison, I would say Dee-Dee's were the size of softballs and mine were the size of golf balls. This is probably why I didn't get into golf growing up and why I don't like it now.

As I was continuing to reflect, I remember the summer I thought I was finally on the team. We moved to College Park, Georgia, and the school I was going to attend also hosted kindergarten through eighth grade. I met two boys. One was named George, whose birthday was the same as mine, and he lived across the street from me. The other was named Ray. Ray was a year older and very cute. Yes, he was a year older and in the eighth grade but who cares. He was cute. He lived in another apartment complex down the street. He was light-skinned, curly-haired, and a football player. George looked like one of the kids from the Addams family, played no sports, was on the thick side, and a nerd. Of course I fell for the athletic one. One day, during lunch, I was throwing the football around with other boys and Ray walked over to me and started talking.

"Hey! I ain't never seen a girl throw a football like that. Where'd you learn?" he asked.

"My brothers taught me," I responded.

"What grade you in?" he asked.

"Eighth," I said. "You?"

"I'm in the eighth grade too but I've haven't seen you before."

"We just moved here from Atlanta. My name is Laura."

"I'm Ray," he said with confidence. "Nice to meet you."

I continued to play catch until lunch was over. I noticed Ray was watching me throw and I made sure he saw just how good I was each time. After school, Ray saw me walking on the high school campus. My sister Dee-Dee and I had to walk home together.

"Hey! Where you goin'?" he yelled from across the parking lot.

"I have to walk home with my sister," I said.

"You got a sister that go here?"

"Yes. And a brother too," I shouted back. Dee-Dee met me most of the way so I wouldn't have to walk so far. Ray decided to start up a conversation with her.

I STUFF MY BRA... *SO WHAT?*

"What's your name?" he asked.

"Della. My friends call me Dee-Dee," she said.

"You pretty," he said.

Dee-Dee didn't flinch. I guess she was used to this by now. I wasn't. I tried bringing the conversation back to me but Ray had seen the light. He was stuck on my big sister and I, again, was standing in her shadow. Once we reached our street, we had to break off from Ray.

"See you tomorrow," Ray said.

"Bye, Ray!" I said in return but he wasn't talking to me. Dee-Dee gave a courtesy wave and kept walking. I didn't talk to her the rest of the way home. I was mad. She stole my boyfriend. When I got home, George was standing at my front door, waiting for me.

"Hi, Laura," he said. "You wanna go swimming later?"

"No. I don't wanna swim with you, you frog," I said in a mean tone.

"You a dog anyway. I was tryin' to be nice," George said.

"Go away, George." I went inside and closed the door behind me.

* * * * *

A few weeks later, it had been so hot in College Park that going swimming was warranted. My mom was at work and my brother Vincent was home with me. As long as I had my homework done and my shower before my mom got home, I would be fine. A little sidenote: in between the time Ray first met my sister and now, he had attempted to holler at her several times with no success.

While my brother and I were swimming, George and his little brother got into the pool too. I was swimming in the deep end when I felt someone touch my behind. It was George *and* his little brother.

"Did you touch me?" I asked.

"No," he said with a smirk on his face.

"If you touch me again, I will kill you," I told them.

"You ain't gon' do nothin'," he replied.

At this time, my brother Vincent was sitting on the steps of the shallow end, watching all of this transpire.

"Touch me again and I will kill you!" I said with certainty.

My brother was throwing little things in the water for me to dive for when I felt someone touch me again. This time, they tried to pull my bikini bottom down. George and his brother were laughing when I came up for air. Because George was the closest to me, I reached over and grabbed him by his neck. I placed him in a headlock, pushed and held his head underwater for about ten seconds. He broke loose and got out of the pool. I followed him out and began fighting him. He tried to pull my bikini top down this time and I was livid. I grabbed him again, got him in a headlock, and started punching him in the face. I could hear George yelling stop and his little brother crying and screaming at me.

"Let my brother go! Let him go!" he screamed. I didn't care. I was mad. I was trying to kill him.

"Git him, lil sister!" my brother shouted. "Hahahaha! That's what you git, boi!" he said.

"Let him go!" the little brother continued. "I'm gonna tell my mom!"

George's little brother ran to get help. About two minutes later, their mother came to the fence that surrounded the pool and yelled at me.

"Little girl! Did you hit my son?" she shouted.

"Yes, ma'am. I did!" I shouted back to her. "He and his brother tried to pull off my bathing suit two times. I told them if they touch me again, I was going to kill them so I tried to drown him!"

"George! You and your brother git in the house. Don't play with that lil' girl no mo! You hear me?" she fussed.

"Yes, ma'am!" they answered.

"Ahhh! George got beat up by a girl!" my brother shouted!

"Go on home, you sissy!" I shouted. "You lucky your momma showed up!"

I got out of the pool and went home. I was hungry now. Fighting worked up my appetite. Around seven o'clock that evening, I noticed Ray was in the pool. He didn't live in our complex and the rule was that each swimmer had to live in the apartment complex in order to swim, but it didn't matter because the superintendent was not around.

"I'm going swimming again. You wanna come?" I asked my brother Vincent.

"No. I'm tired," he said. "Don't be out there long. You know what Madea said," he reminded.

When I got to the pool, I noticed Dee-Dee was there. Ray was trying to talk to her but she was ignoring him. *How had she gotten past me?* I thought. Nonetheless, I had to follow through. As I jumped in the water, I did a cannonball near them, splashing water on her hair. Dee-Dee was very angry with me. Ray laughed as she left the pool. The sun was getting lower. Since she was gone and it was just the two of us, he "decided" to talk to me.

"Hey! I wanna tell you something," he said.

"Yeah? What do you want?" I asked.

"I like you," he said.

"Me?" I responded.

"Yeah, you," he assured me. "Let's play a game," he said.

"What kind of game?"

"A spelling game."

Now I was, after all, the second place winner in the school spelling bee so this was right up my alley.

"Fill in the blank," he said.

I thought this was a spelling game but okay.

"I want to have ____ with you," he said.

"How many letters in the blank space?" I asked.

"Three," he said.

"Is it *eat*? I asked reluctantly. I knew what he wanted but played along. I was alone and half-naked in a pool with a boy older than me, and my big brother was not around. As I headed toward the steps in the shallow end, I finally spelled it right.

"You want to have sex with me?" I asked.

"Yes," he said while grabbing my arm.

"No. Thank you," I responded. "I'm waiting for marriage. Plus my momma would kill me and you."

"Are you sure?" he asked.

"I'm sure," I responded.

My feelings were hurt but I didn't let him see it on my face. As I as leaving the pool, I saw my mom's car pass by. It was dark out. I hadn't had my shower. My homework was not done. I was half-naked, talking to a boy outside, and my hair was full of chlorine. I ran through the backdoor, up the stairs, into the shower, and started my water. I was amazed at how quickly my mom got in the house. I came out of the shower wrapped in a towel to find my mother in my bedroom behind the door.

"Laura Ann?" she said.

"Yes, ma'am?" I said as I turned around.

"Why are you just now taking your shower? Is your homework done?"

So many questions coming at me all at once, I didn't know which to answer first.

"I was outside in the pool. No, ma'am," I said to her.

"Go get my belt," she said.

I didn't want a whoopin' but if I told her what really happened with George, his brother, and his mother, then Ray, it would be worse than that. My mother did not support violence, lying, cheatin', or stealin'. Before she gave the first hit, she asked me where Dee-Dee and my brother Vincent were.

"Dee-Dee is asleep and Vincent is next-door playing the piano."

My guess is she didn't want any witnesses. She hit me five times, and because I was wet, it felt like twenty times.

"Get in there and wash your hair. When you are done, do that homework and wash them dishes!"

"It's Dee-Dee's night!" I cried out.

"Now it's your night!" she demanded.

I quietly did as I was told. While I was in the shower, I asked God why did I get punished for something I didn't do? But then realized I was being punished for something I *didn't* do—my chores and homework. I didn't see Ray anymore after that night. I guess he found another prospect. George and his family moved away two months later.

I STUFF MY BRA... *SO WHAT?*

The following morning, I ran into the bathroom early as I'd done before so I could get dressed. I didn't want my siblings to see my new body. I tried yet another trick to stuffing my bra. I had learned my lesson about the tissue paper so I didn't go back to that. This time, I used real paper. I balled it up and stuffed it inside. As I approached the front steps of the school, I heard one of the boys named Darryl talking.

"What the hell?" he shouted!

"Why are you shouting?" I asked.

"What is wrong with your shirt? he asked.

I looked down, and to my horror, my bumps were now pricklies. The balled-up paper showed through my shirt and had many different points on them. I ran to the bathroom, crying all the way there. I'd failed again! *God, why must you make me wait so long?* I thought. I went to the office and asked the nurse to call my mom so I could go home. I told her I had cramps. My mother couldn't leave work so she gave me permission to walk home. When I arrived home, I took a hot bath. I was thankful I was home alone. And I was thankful it was Friday. I had given up on God and given up on trying to grow boobs.

I had decided not to care about competing with boys at sports or anything else anymore. I buried myself in my studies, playing football, running track, playing soccer, and singing in the choir. I even took a shop class to learn how to work on cars. Boys were everywhere and I didn't care. I didn't care that they looked at me like I was a boy. I dared them to try to say anything to me about my lack of development but none did. I grew mean and took it out on every boy I met. My communication with Ricky was slim to none. He called often but I didn't want to talk to him. I was angry. Even though he'd been the only boy who loved me for me, I turned away.

We visited my granny a few times since we'd left Alabama. I didn't contact Ricky while I was there. I spent most of my time with Mr. and Mrs. Nelson and playing their organ. We shared lemonade and peanut butter and apple jelly sandwiches. When Ricky learned that I had been there and didn't call him, he broke up with me. I was happy about it because now, I didn't have to deal with him. He called me two days later to apologize and ask if I'd be his girl again. I told him no and hung up the phone. He continued calling me once a week.

"What did you do to that boy to make him call you so much, Laura?" my uncle asked.

"Nothing. He's just annoying," I said.

The time spent in Georgia was hard for me. Transitioning to a new school, new home, and new friends made me want to withdraw. Everything else about me was changing as well. Everything but my chest. I wasn't praying to God as much because I felt He wasn't answering my prayers. Dee-Dee had a boyfriend who loved her, and my brother Vincent had several girlfriends that loved him. The older siblings who were sent ahead were now in high school and doing fine. Even though I hated it, I was ready for a change. Even though I wasn't satisfied with my growth, I slowly began to embrace what I knew to be true. While walking home with a few friends, some of them were boys, one of the boys my age began to tease me. It was almost the end of the year and I wore a bright yellow and navy-blue-striped short set that I saved especially for this day.

"Hey, Laura!" I heard one of them call my name.

"What?" I answered and turned around.

"I see your boobs are still lopsided. You still stuffin' your bra?" he asked.

"Actually, dummy. My health teacher, Mrs. Tate, said women's breasts aren't the same size at all. It's natural to have one bigger than the other. And there's nothing wrong with it," I said with confidence.

I stuck my tongue out at him and turned my back to them. I was glad those facts were given to me just in time because on this day, I decided to stuff 'em one more time, hoping no one would notice. *He's stupid anyway*. I thought to myself.

Once I got home, I emptied my bras, changed clothes, and made myself a sandwich. That's when Madea called another family meeting.

"We're moving again!" she said.

"What? Why?" Dee-Dee asked.

"We are going back to California. I haven't been happy here for over a year," Madea said.

"What about my boyfriend!" Dee-Dee asked.

"Who cares!" I shouted. "When do we leave?"

"Shut up you flat-chested cat!" she replied. My face twisted up at her name-calling.

"What about my school? Vincent asked.

"They have schools in California," Madea replied.

What Vincent was really concerned with were all of his girlfriends. I, on the other hand, rejoiced!

"We will move at the end of the school year," she said.

Since we were on the East Coast, this meant school was out in May. It was already mid-April.

Dee-Dee ran to our bedroom to call her boyfriend. She'd been dating him for over two years now. They were really serious. Vincent left the house to pay a few "friends" a visit. My other brothers who'd gotten to Atlanta before us decided to stay since they were almost adults and my uncle said they could stay with him. Madea didn't fight them on it. My mother sold her car because we needed the money. We were set to ride the Greyhound bus to the West Coast. Moving day couldn't come fast enough for me. Before we left, Dee-Dee's boyfriend stopped by the house to say goodbye. He didn't stay long. Just long enough to give her a ten-page letter. I know because I read it. He also handed her a silk red rose. Vincent said his goodbyes the week prior. My friends said goodbye a few days before we left. Our aunt and uncle gave us a ride to the bus station. They hugged us and said goodbye.

Vincent sang all the way to California. It didn't bother me because I was ready to go. Dee-Dee cried all the way there. I went to her seat to support her like she did for me a few years prior but she wouldn't respond. All she did was cry more.

"Don't worry. You'll love California," I said.

"No, I won't!" she replied through her tears. I held Dee-Dee's hand until she fell asleep. I remembered all of what I'd gone through in Alabama and Georgia. God was preparing me for a life change that only He could orchestrate.

* * * * *

The next few years of high school was filled with me having a lack of confidence in myself and who I was unless I was singing. I joined choir at church, the show choir in school, and played basketball as well as joined the band. I looked like Michael Jackson in his awkward years. I wore a Jheri curl afro daily. I didn't wear makeup because it was too much trouble. Boys and girls were more brutal in high school. They knew bigger words and meaner phrases. I was compared regularly with other black girls who seemed to have the patent on growing breasts. I remembered the falsies Mrs. Nelson told me of but Madea didn't wear them anymore and my aunt didn't need them. I was still teased for my flat chest. And one girl said I had gnats in my hair all the time. Didn't she know they were attracted to the Jheri juice? I tried my best to drown it out.

I had a boyfriend in tenth grade as well as the eleventh and twelfth grade. Both relationships failed. During my eleventh and twelfth grade year, that particular boyfriend made it his mission to point out all my flaws and my lack of development. He was not only verbally abusive but physically as well. As I look back on this time, I realize he had serious control issues and lacked a healthy mother-son/father-son relationship. During this time, I felt I couldn't tell anyone. I remember a time when this particular boyfriend and I were getting ready to go get something to eat. My boyfriend allowed his best friend to sit in the front and I had to ride in the back. I shared my opinion with him about it. A few days later, my boyfriend invited me over to this house. When I arrived, I found a note in the screen door telling me to enter through the side door. As I entered, I found another note on top of a heart-shaped pillow that read, "Turn around!" As I turned to see what was there, I felt the left side of my face burning. He had punched me in the face wearing a boxing glove.

"Don't ever disrespect me again!" he said.

I was shocked and my head hurt.

"What?" I asked.

"You disrespected me in front of my best friend the other day when we were getting into the car. Don't do it again!"

After the slap and my shock, he made me have sex with him. I don't have to tell you what that's called. My heart was crushed yet God was still there. My choir director ended up being one of the father figures I needed to guide me in the right direction during school hours. I withdrew from friends because my boyfriend didn't want anything or anyone to take the attention away from him. Singing was what kept me smiling, even though I was hurting. Dee-Dee was still missing her first love from Atlanta but she'd found new friends who seemed to help her get stronger. Vincent had long since gotten over his exes from the East Coast and thrived in choir and the band as well. I just wanted to graduate and die.

"When is your plan gonna kick in God?" I asked reluctantly.

As my senior year progressed, I thought about what to do after graduation. I had gotten sick with pneumonia during the last weeks of school. In fact, I graduated while I was sick and went to grad night as well. I didn't want to miss out. I hated being sick. Mostly because I lost fifteen pounds and the little bit of chest I had was now back to golf balls. All I could do was sigh and shrug my shoulders on how life was going for me. *Surely college will be different,* I thought to myself.

WONDERBRAS

*Fancy underwire, push-up bra that is
flexible, breathable, and stylish.*

I attended the local junior college after graduation. I enrolled in sixteen units of music. I was curious about college life and excited to start something new. Honestly I was bored and wanted to get away from home to gain some independence. I was the last one at home. Dee-Dee had gotten married right out of high school. Vincent moved back to Atlanta. Now I was alone and flat-chested.

While attending my classes, I met a guy from Spain. He was adorable, and he had a beautiful first tenor voice. He was seven years older than me but I didn't care. Neither did he at first. We spent much of our time going out to eat and singing duets in class. I had never heard a more intriguing singing voice before. He took me shopping, and during the summer, he bought me a red polka-dotted bikini. I felt special. I no longer cared about my lack of development in the chest area. He'd made me feel I was enough. The last I'd spoken to Ricky was in the eleventh grade. He called my grandmother and she gave him my current phone number. I was shocked to hear from him. He said he still loved me and missed me. I told him thank you.

After eight months of spending time with my Spaniard, he was preparing to pop the question. It was my birthday week and he said he had a surprise for me. We went to dinner, and on the way home, we talked about general things. He pulled up in front of our condo and turned off the car. He turned to me to speak.

"Laura, I'd like us to get more serious," he said.

"Really? How serious?" I asked.

"I would like to have sex with you," he stated.

"Sex?" I responded as if I'd never heard of it before. I hadn't even kissed him yet, I thought.

"Yes! Sex!" he replied. "Do you have a problem with it?"

"I don't have a problem with it but my momma does," I responded. "I don't want to have sex until I'm married. I want to honor God with my body," I said.

"Hmm," he said. "That's what men and women do when they get closer."

"Really?" I asked, as if I didn't have a brain, and cocked my head to the right.

"Yes," he replied.

"I'm sorry but I can't. I'm waiting for marriage."

"Are you willing to be flexible, Laura?" he asked.

"Nope!"

"Well, I guess you're not a woman after all," he said.

He told me I could keep the items he'd bought for me, kissed me on my cheek, told me to get out of his car, and said goodbye. I sat in the car for about thirty more seconds, pondering on what just happened, opened my door, said goodbye, and then walked in the house. He drove off quickly as if to signify his disappointment in me. I tried reaching out to him a few days later, but he ignored my calls and dropped out of the classes we shared. That night, I wrote in my journal about all of that happened. I cried for about an hour in the tub. I got out, put on my pajamas, and lay in my bed, looking at the moon. I wondered why God had allowed me to be hurt this way. Surely He remembered my past dealings with boys in junior high and high school. Surely He knew this was coming.

"Why didn't you warn me, God? Why aren't I enough just the way that I am?" I asked.

Ricky was brought to mind and I felt worse than before. A few weeks later, I felt strong enough to approach my Spanish ex-boyfriend on campus. Prior to approaching him, I had come up with a plan to stuff my bra differently. This time, I wore several bras—five to be exact—including one of my sister's Wonderbras.

"Hello," I said to him.

He looked at me as if we'd never met.

"Hi," he replied.

"How are you?" I asked.

"I'm fine," he replied.

"Good," I said.

"You look different," he stated while looking at my breast.

"I do?" I asked.

"Yes, you do. Have you changed your mind about our relationship and what I asked?"

"No."

"Okay. See you!" he said.

That was the gist of our conversation. There was nothing else to wonder about with him. I had not been enough girl or woman for him. That change made only a small difference in how he looked at me. The gifts were used to sway me into giving in. He wasn't interested in the north. He wanted what was down south and nothing more. It was his plan all along. But God had another plan and I was thankful He did. Being around him didn't hurt as much as it did the last time we'd spoken. In fact, I was now empowered to share what I'd learned.

In my opinion, Wonderbras were designed to allow the beholder to wonder what was under the shirt. With this newly discovered deception device, women often paid big money to make men think they had what they wanted. Since this new bra made my ex-boyfriend's eyes open up, maybe it will work on others, I thought.

After my adventurous time with my ex, I decided to concentrate on school. I was given my first whistling solo with this choir. I practically begged our director to let me do it. Unfortunately I decided to swallow a small piece of gum, just a few bars, before my debut and not a sound came out. My lips were pursed and my director kept looking at me with a puzzled look on his face. I was embarrassed, to say the least. I have been participating in choirs since I could talk and one of the main disciplines we are taught is to never sing with gum in your mouth. Had I been a few shades lighter, the audience would have been able to see my face turn red. After the show, my director had a few words for me.

"What happened? You begged me for that solo!"

"I swallowed my gum just before the solo. I'm so sorry!" I said.

"I don't understand. You said you were ready."

He sounded so disappointed in me. I began to cry.

"Why are you crying?" he asked.

"Because I let you and the choir down! I failed!" I said through my sobs.

"You didn't let me down, Laura. Only the choir knew there was a solo part there. The audience was clueless. It's just a lesson in life that until you really know you're ready for such a challenge, don't try it." He could see I was sad.

"Look, the rest of the choir members have been singing with me for years. You're the youngest in the group so you have much to learn. From now on, let me lead the choir. When you're ready, I'll know it. You still have my support but you need more discipline."

"Thank you, Mr. T."

I ran to hug him but he extended his hand for a shake instead. He walked out of the room. While I was reliving my blunder in my head, I heard a familiar voice.

"What happened to you out there?" the Spaniard said.

"I swallowed my gum just before my solo," I said in shame.

"Hahahaha. I told you. You're still a little girl!"

I walked over to him and punched him in the chest.

"What was that for?" he asked.

"For being dumb!" I replied.

I walked out of the room and went to stand near some of my real friends. After the event, my friends and I went to dinner. I guess they figured I was shamed enough so no one mentioned the error I'd made. The rest of the night was a blur for me. As I lay in bed again, I wondered what was going on with me. I thought back to being rejected by my ex and how it made me feel. I shook my head, rolled over, and called Dee-Dee.

"Hello?" she answered.

"Hey! What are you doing? How's the baby?" I asked.

"He's fussy tonight. What you callin' for?" she asked.

I told her what happened with my ex and the botched solo and how I wish I could be more like her—faultless.

"I'm not faultless. I got pregnant just out of high school, I'm not working, and now I'm married. Whoopie!"

"Yeah, but you love him and he loves you. That's worth it, right?"

"I guess. Look, I gotta go to bed. I've been up all day with the baby. Don't stress out about boys. They're all dumb, and when they become men, it doesn't really change much. Just be you. You'll get bigger boobs someday and you won't have to worry. Talk to you later, little sis."

Did she just say what I thought she said? As if I needed another reason to cry. That night, I prayed for God to convict my ex so bad he couldn't sleep and he would apologize to me. For Dee-Dee, I prayed the baby would wake up in an hour and keep her up until sunrise. Then I repented, asked for forgiveness, and cried myself to sleep. Surely tomorrow *has* to be better.

The next day, I only had one class. I arrived early and waited outside. I heard someone playing music. I followed the sound, and when I entered the room, I saw an African-American male playing the flute. He stood 6'1" tall and weighed about 140 pounds. The music he played was beautiful. He saw me looking at him.

"Hello," he said.

"Hi," I replied. "I'm Laura. That was beautiful."

"My name is Founts. And thank you."

"I've never seen a black person playing the flute before. How long have you been playing?"

"About ten years," he said.

We continued to exchange pleasantries and I noticed my next class was about to begin.

"I have to go. Nice meeting you," I said.

"Same to you," he said. "Come by tomorrow so we can talk more."

"I will," I replied.

I left the room with a smile on my face. I was shocked that he actually looked me in the eyes the whole time we talked. The next day, we met in the same room as before. We talked about our families, friends, and what careers we wanted. He was kind of nerdy and said he wanted to be a concert flautist. I told him I was going to school to get from under my mom's thumb and every class I was enrolled in has to do with music. We started dating, and after a few weeks, he took me home to meet his parents. They were really nice people. Both had a formal education and spoke nothing but kind words about their son. Founts had a concert in a few days and invited me to attend. I did. We had great chemistry, and he had a sincere heart. There were times I wondered when he was going to break my heart as the others had done before. It seemed too good to be true. We went out for dinner after the concert and he told me he had strong feelings for me. Like teenagers, we walked and talked and smiled senselessly at one another.

A few months later, sensing the day of hurting me was coming soon, I started to pull away from him. I didn't return his calls and began to ignore him at school. Many times, he tried to reach out to me for answers, but out of the fear of possible rejection, I just told him I couldn't see him anymore. I could see his feelings were really hurt because of me. I stopped going by the music room where he practiced in an effort to make things better. Only they got worse.

A few days later, I saw him in the band room practicing. I felt a tug at my heart and decided to go speak to him. He stared right through me and continued playing the flute. I looked down out of shame, walked away, and skipped my next class. I had hurt another sweet human being for no reason at all. I could see he liked me for who I was, not for what he could get from me. I didn't attend the junior college the following semester and I lost touch with the group

I sang with. A few months later, I tried to reach out to my flute player but his number had changed. I found out he and his parents moved out of state because he got the opportunity to play professionally. I did not drink alcohol back then, but if I had, that would have been a great day to get drunk. It took me months to get over the guilt of hurting him, losing a great friend, and possibly a promising future with him. I had been given another Ricky Jones and I blew it!

I got my first job working with my mom in a factory. I gave up school altogether to make money and move on. I never told Dee-Dee about him. I didn't want to hear her disappointment in me. I couldn't take that right now. Life was a little better now but I missed the flute player. For the next decade or so, I would reflect on my choices in relationships, get more involved in church activities, have some children and get married—not necessarily in that order. I was hoping this new choice would be much better than the past ones.

FILLER BRAS: I WANT MY MOMMY!

It was now the middle of June in the year 2001. I was married now and my family and I were preparing to take our first family vacation across the country. We had plans to visit all of our relatives on the Southeast coast and introduce our kids to another part of the United States. Our minivan was eighteen months old but it still needed some greasing of the gears. And what better way to do that than to drive to Mississippi, Alabama, and Georgia? Approximately two years before, I begged my ob-gyn to refer me to have a mammogram. Though the golf balls were now oranges, my breasts were always sore and Lord knows I was done having kids so I know it was not because of pregnancy nor was my monthly visitor on her way. Because of my age—thirty-three—doctors would not give me mammogram referrals in the past because of the density of the breast tissue. I knew cancer was rampant in my family. Other families had good genes, good hair, and good skin. We had lung cancer, brain cancer, stomach cancer, liver cancer, and breast cancer. I insisted that I get checked to at least rule out cancer and find out what the problem was. Finally I received a referral. I called the mammography department and scheduled an appointment. I had to go alone because my spouse was working and my mother was dealing with cancer herself and was too weak to accompany me.

Once I was done swimming through piles of paperwork that asked the same questions in different ways at the front desk, I went into the women's waiting room. This room was as pink as pink gets. Pink cancer ribbons were everywhere. They were on the walls, clipboards, the doors, even on the light poles. I was so fascinated that I just stood there with my mouth open. I found my way to the undressing room and followed the instructions on the wall, "Please wear gown with the opening to the front if you are here for a mammogram. If you are here for a bone density scan, please wear your gown with the opening toward the back."

I proudly slipped on my gown and walked out with my clothes in my hand. The sign didn't tell me to close the gown as I exited to undressing room so all of my goodies were peeking out. I was proud to be part of the club now where no one had to wonder if I was a male or female. I quickly covered myself with my own clothing, sat down, and waited to be called by the technician. I prayed it would be a woman—it was. She took me into this room where there were many white machines with knobs, glass, and cabinets with labels on them. I struggled with the technician to remove my arm out of the gown. I thought to myself, *She has no business touching me like this*. But I quickly found out that this was part of the procedure.

The technician sensed my fear and uncertainty about what was about to transpire and she told me to relax and let her do all the work. Again I thought to myself, *Are we still doing a mammogram?* I prayed in my head that this would go quickly. As the technician handled me and placed my breasts on the cold plastic item that looked like a container to reheat my lunch in, she then turned this knob and another piece of the container came down and smashed my breast. I started crying because it was slightly painful and I was afraid of what they might find. The technician told me to hold my breath and to stay still. The next thing I heard was a buzzer and the machine let go of me. I had to go through this five more times, two on the left side and three on the right side. All I wanted to do was cry out for my mom. I wanted to be with her so bad at this moment. When the technician was done, she told me to go into the waiting room and not to get dressed. Five minutes passed and she came out to apologize for the discomfort and told me I was free to leave. I couldn't get dressed fast enough. I wiped my tears, got dressed, and literally ran to my car.

My mind was now on my first family vacation. I told my mother of my experience with the mammogram machine and she couldn't stop laughing. It wasn't funny to me though. My mother and I discussed the intentions of our family trip and then we had lunch. After all, getting your boobies smashed worked up an appetite in a girl.

A few days before we were to leave on our vacation, I received a phone call from the mammography department. They needed to take another picture of my left breast. The technician made a mistake. I informed the technician that I was leaving and it would have to wait until I returned. We were set to return on August 2, and my good friend was getting married August 4. I didn't want anything to get in the way of me being one of her bridesmaids so I scheduled my follow-up mammogram for the eleventh of August.

Our vacation was great! We were able to visit and enjoy many relatives from both sides of the family. Our kids had a ball seeing the country. The thought of my exam or results never entered my mind. I was determined to have fun. And I did. This was one of the greatest memories I have of me and my family. The vacation and my friend's wedding were now behind us. My follow-up mammogram was in the next few days. I proudly strutted to the registration desk, then to the pink room, got undressed, and prepared for my next exam. Just like the one before, I was asked to wait in the front room until the technician gave me the green light to go home. And just like before, she said I was free to leave; but this time, I had to take my X-rays with me to another doctor in the radiology department. I took the long walk to radiology and handed in my films. I was asked to wait about twenty minutes. I called my husband to check in and let him know what was going on, and then the radiologist came out and said I could leave. I left happily because I thought everything was fine. I jumped into my car and drove home.

Reflecting on the fun we'd had in the past month kept me company on my drive. Unfortunately the memory of a wonderful family vacation and my friend's wedding was overshadowed by a phone call. When I returned home, a message was left on our answering machine. It was the radiologist. I returned his call immediately. I was downstairs in the kitchen when I returned his call. My children were in the living room, watching television. Our conversation went something like this:

"Hi. This is Laura Franklin returning your call."

"Yes, Mrs. Franklin," he said with sad assuredness. "Thank you for returning my call. We have discovered something in your mammogram. It looks like it is precancer and we need to schedule you for a lateral breast biopsy so we can confirm our suspicions. Nonetheless, whatever it is, we need to get it out and we need to get it out now! I have scheduled you for a biopsy tomorrow morning at 10:00 a.m. Can you make it?"

"Uh, yes I can. When and where did you say?" Blah, blah, blah, blah, blah was all I heard from him but I somehow managed to write all of this information down.

"Okay, doctor. Thank you and see you then."

I immediately ran upstairs, skipping several on my way up. I could hear my kids calling out to me, asking me why I was running in the house when we've told them a million times not to do so. I closed my bedroom door, knelt down at the foot of my bed, and began crying and praying. All I remember is a faint battle cry coming from inside but I couldn't hear it on the outside.

With my mind racing, I thought, *Precancer? That's like being prepregnant. Either I have it or I don't. This is nuts*! I began to pray out loud.

"Lord, I know you're the Creator of everything and you know what's going on inside me. But, Lord, whatever it is, I want it out and I want it out now! Please, Lord, take it out!"

I continued crying, but now, I was sitting on the floor surrounded by laundry. I felt I should be praying on my knees so I rested on my knees again at the foot of my bed.

"I need my mommy. I want my mommy!" I shouted.

I STUFF MY BRA... *SO WHAT?*

With tears running down my face, again, I asked God to remove this poison from my body.

"Why me, Lord?" I asked.

"Why not you?" I heard the Holy Spirit ask.

Then I could feel my body begin to rock back and forth and a sense of peace came over me. This was a significant motion for me because when I was a little girl, my granny, my mom, and big sister used to rock me to sleep. It was used to calm me when I got scared. I knew my question had been answered and I knew it was nothing but God who rocked me. As soon as I finished praying, I got up and made some phone calls. I don't remember who I told first because now I was on autopilot. Nothing else mattered except for me to have the biopsy. I did laundry, got the kids situated for the evening—dinner and bathed—then I prepared for my appointment. My mother could not go with me because she still wasn't feeling well. Little did I know she was going through her second battle with cancer, and this time, the prognosis was more serious.

My husband accompanied me to the biopsy appointment. I was told not to have on any lotions or perfumes and I couldn't wear deodorant. I felt plain. I took my coloring book and crayons with me. My way of relieving stress was to color. While my husband and I waited, I colored at least two full pages. I was nervous and anxious. I'm not quite sure what my husband was feeling. Maybe he was a little nervous too. During this time, our marriage was already facing challenges. Our relationship was strained due to a myriad of reasons. We loved each other, but at this point, we were more or less tolerating each other.

My name was called and I jumped up. My husband could not enter the room with me. I handed my things to him, walked in, and they closed the door behind me. I'm sure it was my imagination but the sound of the door closing reminded me of a jail cell door slamming; not that I've ever been in jail but I've seen it on television. The room was full of machines, bright lights, and a lot of junk I didn't recognize. The table I was to lay down on for the procedure was padded and it had a hole in it almost near the top. This hole was for me to stick my breast in while I lay on my stomach. I smiled immediately because this table could be of service at home. Because I said this out loud, the nurses laughed at me and said I had been the first to ask to borrow it. There was way too much tension in the room so I had to make a joke.

I had the sweetest nurses. One was young, about my age, and the other was about sixty years old. I tried to get the lay of the room while they were asking me questions. I wanted to know what every button did. This was *my* life here. I should know what's going to happen to me, right?

"What type of music do you like?" the older nurse asked.

"Gospel music," I replied.

The younger nurse immediately put on a song that I knew. The older nurse began to give me instructions.

"Lie facedown with your breast in the hole," she said. "You will feel pinches, tugs, pulls and hear loud noises but do not be afraid. The doctor is going to place a small locator chip in your breast for the doctor when he does surgery. This is to ensure he removes the tissue from the correct area as well as the surrounding tissue."

The doctor had entered the room now and she was preparing to numb my entire breast. The older nurse stood next to me by the table, rubbing my arm for comfort, and the younger nurse assisted the doctor. As soon as the machines began, my tears began to flow. The nurse standing next to me asked me questions to take my mind off of the procedure.

"Why are you crying?" she asked.

"I'm scared," I replied through a shaky voice.

"God has everything under control," she said. "Angels are watching over you."

That should have made me feel better but it made me cry more. I wanted my mommy! When the doctor was done, I was able to sit up. I realized that not only was the older nurse there to comfort me but she was also there to hide the tool used to numb me and place the locator chip inside my breast. The tool was the size of a caulking gun for the bathtub. I felt sick when I saw it because some of my breast tissue was left on the end. The younger nurse hurried to remove it out of my sight. I was given bathing and driving instructions while my wound healed. Everything seemed to be moving too fast for me. I hugged the ladies, even the doctor, and told them thank you. As my husband and I walked back to the car, he asked me many questions but I don't remember answering any of them. I just wanted to sleep. The biopsy was on August 11, 2001, and I got the phone call with results on August 14, 2001.

When we arrived at the doctor's office to hear the news, we were greeted with confused faces. It may have been my sensitivity to the situation because everyone seemed as if they knew before I did. Even the people in the waiting room looked suspicious. We didn't have a babysitter so we had to bring all five of our kids with us to this appointment. One of the nurses took the boys into the Comfort Room" and the other nurse took me and my husband into a patient room. Our two-year-old daughter, Mara, stayed with us. While we waited, I remember my husband asking me how I was doing. I was annoyed with his questions by now. I didn't want to answer any more of them. I just wanted to know what was wrong and I wanted to be done. The doctor entered the room with a pale look on his face.

"Blah, blah, blah, blah, blah, blah, circle, circle, circle, dot, dot, dot, you have what is called precancer," he said. "It's in the milk ducts. The medical term for it is DCIS. Ductal carcinoma in situ. This means that cancer cells are in the milk ducts, not the lymph nodes, and is not invasive but it is still cancer. It's precancer because it's in stage 0."

He went on to tell me the survival rates and that's when everything went black. I couldn't hear a thing. I was holding my daughter and all I could think of was missing out on her and her brothers' futures, my death, and I was angry. The ball in my throat was so large I felt as if I were suffocating. I felt my body reach for breath and I was dizzy. What brought me back was the doctor touching my knee and him showing me a diagram of where the cancer cells were. He then asked me if I had any questions. I looked at him as if he told a bad joke.

"Do I have questions?" I asked. "Of course I do, I just can't think of any right now."

The doctor left the room for about a minute, and while he was gone, my husband was talking to me. All I heard was muffled sounds. My daughter was wiping my tears. He took our daughter out of my hands to give me a break. When the doctor returned, he told me my surgery was scheduled for the following week. He mentioned I would be incapable of doing a lot of physical work for at least two to three weeks. I protested because a mother of five couldn't just stop being who she is for a surgery. I needed more time. I told him I had to get my house in order first. Life doesn't stop because I have a diagnosis. My marriage, parenting, and ministry work had to be placed on the back burner. The surgeon checked his calendar and told me the next available surgery date was to be September 14, 2001. I agreed to that date.

After speaking with the surgeon, I was sent to a service coordinator who would give me information regarding bras, surgery options, and more. The woman showed me pictures of women who had double mastectomies, a single mastectomy, and breast reconstruction. Mind you, I was still trying to recover from the doctor's information and now she's giving me surgery options, more statistics of how cancer can return, and my life expectancy. My husband was now in the other room with the kids. The ball in my throat returned and I heard nothing she said to me. She gave me a paper with information, a shopping bag full of pamphlets and books that I did not want to read. In this bag was a brochure on specialty bras with special pockets. I just shook my head, told her thank you, and went to get my kids.

My kids knew immediately that something was wrong because my eyes were very red from crying. My two oldest sons just stared at me with a sad look on their faces. At this time, we felt they were too young to understand and hadn't told them about the cancer. Only that Mommy was sick. My daughter held my hand and our other boys walked with my husband. On our way home, my husband asked me what I wanted to do.

"Ain't no sense in crying," I answered. "I have work to do. I'm going to have the lumpectomy. Let's get busy!" I said to him.

I rolled down my window for some fresh air, and on this day, everything in nature looked more beautiful to me than it had before. I dropped the kids and my husband off at home and went to see my mother to tell her the news. As I told her what the diagnosis was, I lay my head on her bedside, crying.

"Don't worry," she said. "All sickness is not unto death."

I jumped up off the floor so quick it made my head spin. My mother gave me a strange look. I told her she was right. I gave her a kiss, told her thank you, and said goodbye. I then went to the church and spoke to my pastor who gave me some advice on asking more questions to the doctors about recovery and long-term plans. He also gave me multiple scriptures to hold on to, prayed with me, gave me a hug, and told me to keep him informed.

The next few weeks flew by. I was trying to make sure I had babysitters lined up for the kids in case they had to be separated. I stored food in the freezer and plenty of extras just in case. By now, all of my siblings knew and some of my other extended family members. I told only a few of my friends. I didn't want people coming over feeling sorry for me or coming over to gawk at me as if they didn't know what a cancer patient looked like. I also had two women in place to comb Mara's hair. I wanted to be sure she was looking pretty when I wasn't around. My dad called me during this time to check on me.

"Laura?" he said.

"Yes, Dad."

"You okay?"

"I will be. How are you?"

"I'm fine. I'll be praying for you. I love you."

"I love you too, Daddy."

I didn't realize his call was the last thing I needed to hear to stay encouraged. I felt I was going to succeed. There was still more to do but my daddy called, and at that moment, I felt like his little girl and everything would be better than all right.

Words of Encouragement

God gave me this song three years after my first diagnosis of breast cancer in 2001.

He Chose Me

Looking back, I had to face
That you Lord had been replaced
With suffering from all that I had done.
Every time I made a move
You were there to see me through
For nothing. No way I had a clue.
No matter how I treated Him, He always tagged along
I thought I never needed him. I never walked alone.
Chorus:
He chose me. He chose me
When I turned my back and walked away, He still protected me
He chose me. He chose me
In spite of who I am, He chose me.
So I sat and thought to myself. No matter where I go
I can only follow Him and no one else for others they will know
That's the only reason I'm still here is because there's work to do
All of the confusion has been cleared. It's time
to make my move. Serving God is
not a thing of time, it's a lifestyle. Saying that
my life was mine I was acting like a
child.

ANGELS IN MY POCKET: BEAUTY ISN'T SEEN, IT'S SHOWN

I was enrolled in junior college during this time and I had to withdraw from all of my classes. I took a doctor's note with me to explain why I needed a refund for my classes and my books. This was embarrassing and scary.

It was September 11, 2001, and I was getting dressed to head to the college to withdraw from my classes when I received a phone call. It was my mother. She told me to turn on the television. There had been a terrorist attack on the World Trade Center, the Pentagon, and another location. What I was watching was a replay of earlier events because the East Coast is three hours ahead of us. I was saddened but not shaken. I think that's because I was caught up in my own world and how it would be changing in the next few days and I didn't feel the gravity of what occurred.

"Maybe they'll reschedule your surgery until all of this was over," my mom said.

We both knew that wouldn't happen. I got off the phone, got in the car, and headed to the junior college. My first stop was the registration office. I had to withdraw from the classes before I could get my refund for the classes.

"Next in line!" I heard the student behind the counter say.

When the student behind the counter asked me why I was withdrawing, I handed him the paper the doctor gave me. He looked down at my chest and back to my face as if he was looking for the breast to be sticking out or something. I was already ashamed and embarrassed to have to tell him, now this.

"Wait here for a minute," he said. Then he left.

When he returned, he had a woman with him. The woman asked me to come closer to the counter because she had something to tell me. She whispered in my ear the next steps I had to take. She immediately withdrew my name from the class schedules and told me to go downstairs for my refund.

"Good luck and God bless you," she said.

"Thank you," I said to her with a smile. I also told the student thank you as well. He looked at me with sincere eyes and lowered his head.

My second step was the cashier. I went downstairs for my refund, and when I was asked why I was withdrawing, I showed the cashier the note from the doctor.

"Good luck," she said. She immediately handed me a refund, gave me a crooked and sorrowful smile.

"Thank you," I replied. I moved on to the student bookstore.

My third and final step for withdrawing was to see how much money, if anything, I could get back for my books. As I entered the bookstore, I spoke to a male student about my refund. In my mind, I had already told way too many people about my diagnosis.

"May I speak to the manager?" I asked.

"Why?" he replied in a rude tone.

I frowned at him.

"I need a full refund for my books."

"Yeah right!" he responded indignantly. "The manager is not available so you will have to deal with me."

I gave him the paper the doctor gave me. After he read it, just like the other male student, he looked at my chest then up to my face. Maybe I was supersensitive, but when he called for the "unavailable" manager, it seemed louder than it should have been. When the manager came up front, he looked mad. His shoulders were broad and tight.

"How can I help you?" he asked.

I showed him the paper the doctor gave me. His shoulders relaxed instantly. With a heavy sigh, he asked me to step to the side.

"You can't have a full refund because the deadline has passed. You can only get half."

"Half is fine," I replied.

He gave me a form to fill out, explaining why I had to withdraw. While I filled out the form, he began talking to me.

"My wife was diagnosed with breast cancer. The news devastated my family. We'd just had a newborn baby and they were unsure about treatments, surgery, and they were hurting. But no matter what happened, our total trust was in God because He knows best. Make sure you do the same."

"I will. I promise." He gave me half-price for my books.

"I'll be praying for you," he stated.

"I will do the same for you," I told him. We said our thank yous then I left.

I had two more days to myself until my surgery was to be performed. The events of withdrawing from my classes wore me out mentally. The next day, I was scheduled to do my pre-op blood work and paperwork. The nurse I had was very nice and was intentionally gentle with me. She was talking about off-the-wall things but I suspect that it was because of her nervousness about the situation and attempting to make me feel comfortable. Initially her words were just noise to me. Then she said something profound.

"You will be fine."

I looked at her in confusion.

"Thank you."

I left the hospital and felt grateful that God had placed so many people on my path to reassure me that He was with me and in control. For a while, I wasn't worried about what was coming up in the next couple of days. I had to make a phone call to withdraw from running the Los Angeles Marathon that was scheduled for March of 2002. My doctor advised me against it because after surgery and during my radiation treatments, he didn't want the breast tissue disturbed by the rigorous movement. Plus he said it would be very painful for me in the long run. I spoke to a really nice man on the phone regarding my registration. He sounded like an older gentleman.

"It's too late to receive a refund but you could still receive your T-shirt. Why are you withdrawing?"

"I have been diagnosed with breast cancer, my surgery was the next day and my doctor advised against it," I said with a heavy sigh.

"Oh, okay," he said with a chuckle.

I found his response a little insensitive.

"Over forty years ago, my wife was diagnosed with breast cancer and given a 30-percent chance to live through the following year," he said.

"I'm sorry to hear that," I told him.

"I'm not sorry," he responded. "She's probably sorry because she's been stuck with me all these years." I laughed. I was very glad his wife was still alive. "Doctors can be wrong and nobody but God knows when your time is up. You'll be fine and me and my wife will be praying for you. Keep your head up!" I could feel him smiling through the phone.

"Thank you. I will," I said to him.

"God bless you, young lady." Then he hung up the phone.

I had never been surer of God and His decision about my health until now. After I hung up the phone, I went upstairs and grabbed my Bible. I read my favorite passage, Isaiah 41:10. It says, "Fear thou not; for I am with thee: be not dismayed; for I am thy God: I will strengthen thee; yea, I will help thee; yea, I will uphold thee with the right hand of my righteousness" (KJV). No one at that moment could make me believe differently. I prepared myself for the next day, my surgery day. The kids were at my in-laws. I ate an early dinner—something light—took my bath, said my prayers and went to bed with no worries in my head.

A Photo Gallery of My Journey and Dedications

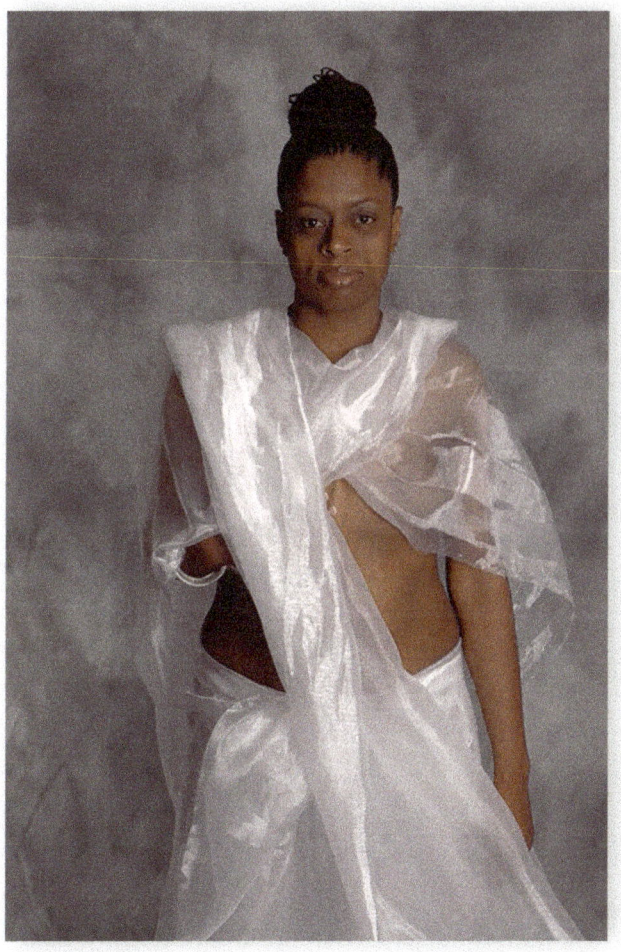

To Anna Sevier, Laura Fonville, Vivian Stephen, Eleanor Drucker, and Genie Garza, you ladies were instrumental in my life. I learned how to fry chicken, be professional in the workplace at all times, smile through *all* challenges, and accept that God's will is what's best for me.

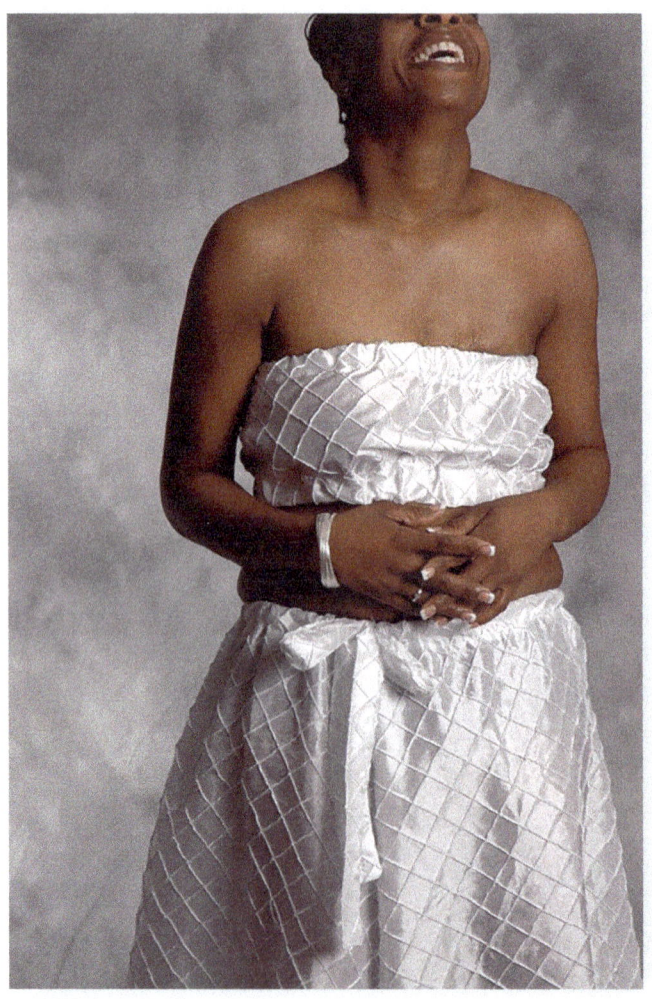

This one is for my number 1 ride-or-die chick—my daughter, Mara. You bring me such joy and make my heart smile. You make me laugh every day—sometimes to tears—and I thank God for your wisdom, your wacky sense of humor, your creativity, strength, and your honesty. I pray we continue to laugh more than we cry. Mommy truly, truly loves and appreciates you.

To my sisters Liz and Yolanda, my scars are beautiful, and it is my prayer that this disease stops with me.

> "I will praise thee; for I am fearfully and wonderfully made: marvelous are thy works; and that my soul knoweth right well" (Psalms 139:14, KJV)

To my bra stuffers, for all the times I tried to be something I wasn't, trying to create something that was not meant for me, trying to fit into a bra not meant for me to wear, I say, "Smile because you are unique! You are enough! God's got you!"

To my crew of sisters: Zelda Adams (not pictured), Rhonda Hill, and Robin Shepherd. Thank you for being there for me during this time. You gave up your entire day to assist me. Rhonda, thank for you the beautiful garments you made for me to wear. I couldn't have pictured it any other way.

To my photographer, Khalil Abdul-Aziz (fondly known to me as Wayne), thank you for being willing to follow the dream I presented to you. Your professionalism, vision, patience, and guidance during this photo shoot made it easier to be vulnerable for the camera, even though it took seven hours for me to relax. You have a true appreciation for beauty, a gentle spirit, and a gift for art.

To Chuck and Rose Heaton, thank you for loving my baby girl and taking good care of her for me while I was going through treatment. Rest in heaven. Forever, my friends.

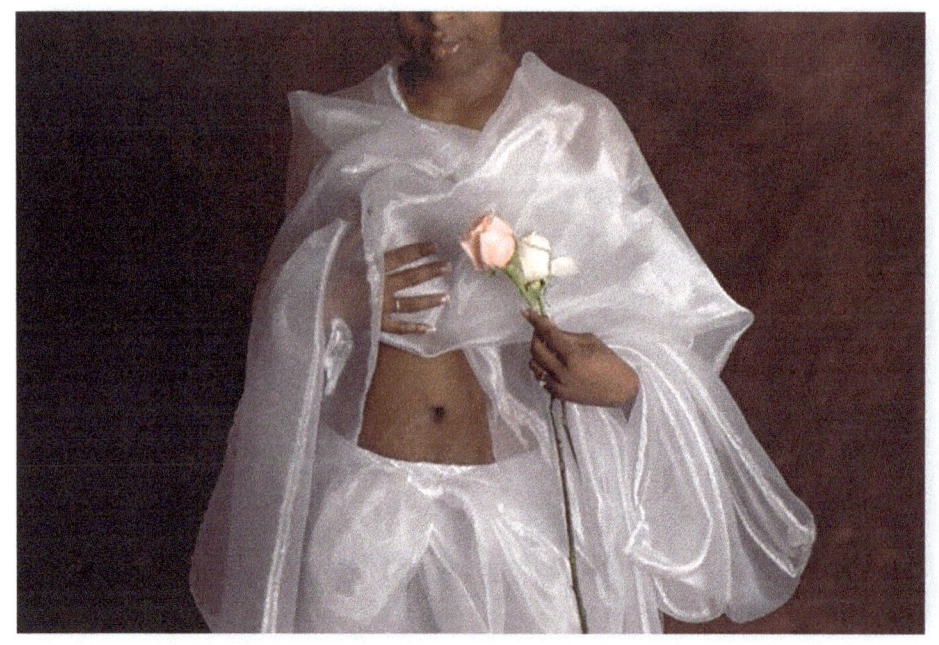

To Ricky Jones, thank you for loving me and seeing me as I was.

To my momma, Eloise, you once gave me this look before I went into my first surgery, September 14, 2001. You kissed me on my cheek, and as you walked away, this is the expression I remember on your face. I knew things would be okay before and after I closed my eyes.

To Pastors G, L, and M, the prayers of the righteous availeth much. You already know.

To all the waterheads that did me wrong.

To my sons Jonathan, Jedidiah Sr., Deion, and Derick, Mama loves you guys so much. You are strong men of God, and though it wasn't easy watching me go through this battle, I am proud of the way you handled everything that came before, during, and after. You are my heroes!

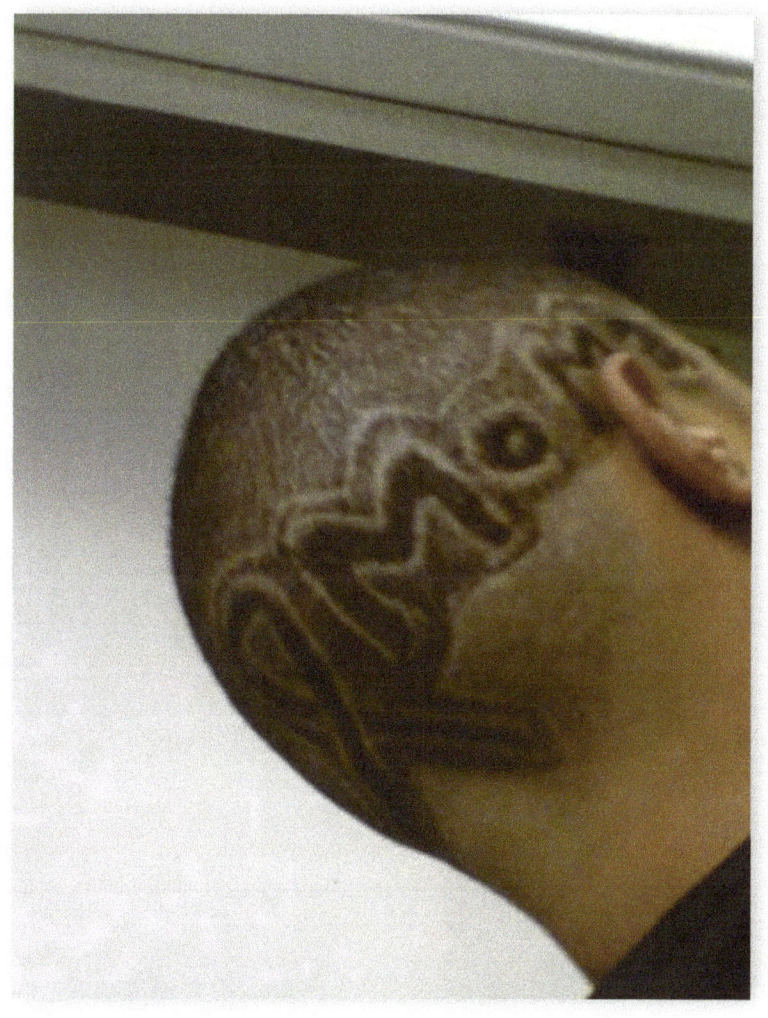

My older boys, Jonathan and Jedidiah Sr., had their hair cut with this design in honor of me and my mom.

MY "D" CUP AND ME: GRACE IS A DIVINE GRATUITY

I had to be at the hospital by 5:00 a.m. the next morning. My husband stayed at home with the kids while my mother took me to the hospital. All I carried with me was my medical card, my crayons, and my coloring book. My mother had her Bible and her purse. I colored a lot while we waited. I can honestly say that I was not afraid of what was to come. One of the main things I didn't like was being put under anesthesia. The rest I could handle.

My name was called and my mother and I walked into the preparation room, holding hands. I was in bed 7. That was a significant number for me. All of the televisions were turned to the news channels. The attack on America was being shown. I changed into a hospital gown with the back out. My mother was asked to leave the area for about fifteen minutes while they put the locator needle in my breast. Because the needle was so long, they covered it with a red Solo cup. History has shown that nothing good goes into a red Solo cup. This cup was placed there so I wouldn't knock the needle out of place. If that happened, the surgeon might cut in the wrong area. I thought it was hilarious because for years, I had wanted bigger boobs, and now, because of this locator needle, I finally had a D cup.

When Pastor M came in to see me and pray with me before they wheeled me out, he frowned. He didn't like hospitals.

"Look, pastor. I'm a D cup!" I said. He just rolled his eyes and so did my mother.

Pastor M, along with my mom and the doctors and nurses who stood around me, prayed for me, and then he left. My sister Yolanda came in to see me as well but left early. She didn't want to see me that way. There were at least fifteen patients waiting for some type of surgery to happen so I did what any red-blooded woman would do—I asked questions.

"What you in for?" I asked one of them. One had cataracts, broken bones, heart trouble, back troubles, and someone was getting something removed.

"Good luck, and I will be praying for y'all!" I shouted.

"Thank you!" they resounded! My mother just shook her head in confusion. I was at peace so I wanted to spread that around.

The anesthesiologist came to my bedside, introduced himself, and gave me small details of the procedure. He told me my nurse would be there shortly to administer the IV. I shook his hand and told him he couldn't leave until we prayed. He agreed to pray with us. The nurse finally showed up and the anesthesiologist said he would see me in the operating room, as if I had somewhere else to be. Unfortunately my nurse was watching the newscast about the attack on America and missed my veins altogether, causing the sleepy juice to spill out. It took her four attempts to get it in. Had she focused on me, it wouldn't have taken so long. I was not happy and I reported her to her superior. I didn't see her anymore after my report.

It was now time for me to be wheeled into the operating room. It was just me, my D cup, and the orderly at first. As he was wheeling me in, I was praying to God silently. I was feeling a little scared. It appeared that the orderly was thinking out loud and said, "Don't worry. You'll be fine," as if God used him to answer me. I looked back at him, and he asked me a question.

"You okay, Laura?"

"Yes. Thank you."

I was feeling pretty sleepy by now. I guess the nurse got it right after all. I heard beeping machines and I was very cold. Everyone in the room ignored me. I kept talking to them but no one answered. The next thing I remember, I was in the recovery room. I was warm. I could hear the nurses talking around me. They tried to wake me up so I could go home, but I knew that if I didn't wake up at a certain time, I would stay for observation. So I faked being asleep until my doctor came in. They alerted him of their inability to wake me up. He came over to my bed.

"Mrs. Franklin. Are you okay?" he whispered to me.

"I'm fine," I whispered back. "I don't want to go home today. I have five children and I want to stay overnight to get some rest."

The doctor agreed to let me stay. I lifted my head from under the covers and smiled at the nurses. From that moment on, I remember our youth minister stopping by to pray for me late in the night and me being hungry. I went home the next day. I was very sore, still hungry, and drained. I slept a lot over the next few days. About a week later, I received a call from the doctor's office, informing me that I had a post-op appointment in another week. When I made it to that appointment, the surgeon removed the bandages and showed me my scar. He was so proud of his work that he smiled like a kid on Christmas.

"Look how beautiful the scar is, Laura!" he said to me. "I am a genius!" he said to me. "The margins were good and clear."

"What does that mean?" I asked.

"When the breast tissue was removed, it was placed in this round, shallow dish. The dish has lines in it with black ink. If the tissue samples stay within the lines in the margin and ink, this means the cancer had not spread to the lymph nodes."

I wanted to see the tissue he removed from my breast. He told me it was downstairs in the lab and that I could see it after my appointment. The surgeon told me I had to do thirty-six radiation treatments as a precaution. These treatments were to be done at a hospital in Hollywood. I had to drive there Monday through Friday and I could not miss any of my appointments. If I missed a treatment, I would have to make it up. But before any treatments were to be done, I had to get another MRI and do blood work to ensure no cancer cells existed in other parts of my body. I called the MRI machine the powder doughnut. I call it this because it's big, white, and round.

This test would take at least forty-five minutes to an hour and I had to lie completely still. The technician wrapped a rubber band around my feet so they wouldn't fall to the side, causing the machine to malfunction. I didn't like this machine because I felt closed in, almost as if I was being buried alive. As my head approached the entry, I saw less light and I felt my heart rate increase. I did not want to do this again so I played a song in my head to distract myself. I was so scared something would be found that I cried during the entire test, but I didn't move. When the test was over, the technician told me to wait on the table. My mind began to wander and I feared the worst. When he returned, he told me I was done. I couldn't get out of there fast enough.

My mind did backflips and cartwheels on the way home. I tried to process everything at once yet I found myself thinking about nothing at all. I wondered what the other doctors and nurses would do to me when I started radiation. I had doubts about all of what I had to do, about if they knew what they were doing, but it was necessary for me to live so I just took a deep breath and did what I had to do.

A month after my surgery, I had an appointment to schedule and fill out paperwork for radiation treatment. I was there for three hours. Once again, I had to be placed in a doughnut—MRI machine. This one was much larger than the first. It was noisier as well. I had to get undressed from the waist up in a room the size of an outhouse. There wasn't much privacy. I could see all kinds of people walking by and it felt like each one of them looked at me through the crack in the door. I guess I was taking too long because the female technician knocked on my door to see if I was okay. Reluctantly I walked out of the outhouse dressing room and followed her into a large room where they kept the big doughnut. The technician took photos of me with an instant camera. She took so many I was feeling a little violated. I was getting a headache and I hadn't even begun the testing. I'm sure it was because of my nerves and anxiety of the moment.

After the photos were taken, she had to put markers on my body. These were little permanent black dots, like tattoos, that were strategically placed on my cancerous breast, rib cage, sternum, and my side. They were there to be sure the radiologist treated the correct areas. She then wrote on my body with blue, black, and white Sharpies. I looked like I was tagged by a preschooler. After I lay down, I was told not to move. At first, it was cool knowing I was doing this. I pretended I was in a spaceship, getting ready to be launched out of a hole or something. But then, it got scary when the table began to move. Tears began to flow down into my ear. My body began quivering because I wanted to get up. I was afraid. I didn't move. It lasted an hour, just as they predicted. I was not allowed to get dressed immediately because the technician needed to be sure she covered everything. Finally I was excused. I couldn't wait to get home and wash off the markings. That night, I remember lying in bed and all I could hear was the sound of the machine going off. I began to cry. In my head, I asked God, *Are you sure*? Then I rolled over and cried myself to sleep.

I showed up for my first radiation treatment. It was awkward for me because I had to tell the receptionist why I was there. Surely they knew, right? I assumed they did. It didn't pay to have an appointment because it took them forever to call my name. Well, fifteen minutes was forever in this situation as far as I was concerned. I was anxious again and wondered what they were going to do to me. I did the usual blood pressure check, weight check, and answered a million questions. Then I was taken to a room in the back where I had to change into a gown, open front, and wait yet again for my name to be called. I heard a young voice say my name. It was the technician who was to give me the treatment. *He has to be at least twelve years old*, I thought. I looked at him as if he was mud. I refused to take off my gown in front of him. I guess he sensed my hesitance because he went to get a female technician to do my treatment. Though she was a female, I was still uncomfortable but I took off the gown. She noticed my marker had been washed off. She left the room and came back with more markers. She told me to lie down on the table and she proceeded to write on me. She wasn't a good artist. Again I had to lie perfectly still to ensure only the correct area was treated. I already hated being there.

This treatment took twenty minutes. When she was finished, I walked as fast as I could to the dressing room, changed my clothes, grabbed my purse, and left. I didn't want to go back anymore. I had no privacy there. No friends. I had been touched by a stranger and I had no one to tell. My drive home was full of tears yet again. I still had thirty-five more treatments to go. I called my mom and told her of my experience.

"God knows," she said. *Was this all she had to say?* I thought.

I bent my face in an ugly way, told her I loved her, and hung up the phone. I was exhausted now and I went to bed very early.

I was now on treatment number 15 or 20. I was a professional! I started walking into the rooms freely exposed with no shame. I was a cancer survivor and I was not going to hide my much prayed-for breasts from anyone. I often laughed to myself. Though I dreaded driving all the way to Hollywood, I dreaded the treatments even more. But the more I went, the less I had in front of me. It was a holiday weekend. Veteran's Day. Up to this point, all of my appointments, I had attended alone. My husband was off work. Both he and the kids came this time. While in the waiting room, we met an older couple. The husband was there because he was diagnosed with prostate cancer. Now I felt ashamed of my ranting about being touched so much and feeling violated. Surely he must be more embarrassed than me—to have to be handled by strangers. We had a good visit with them. Their names were Rose and Chuck Heaton. They had been married for forty-plus years. Chuck said he was going to leave Rose for the young female technician that treated him. We all laughed. This was the first good laugh I'd had in a long time. From then on, Chuck and I had our radiation treatments scheduled at the same time so we could talk.

As the days went by, I shared my coloring book with Rose and Chuck. They liked the idea of using it for therapy. They also took a liking to our daughter. She became their adopted granddaughter.

They spoiled her so much. There was a time when I had to take my daughter with me to treatment because I did not have a babysitter, and with apprehension, I allowed Rose and Chuck to watch her for me.

"Go on, Mommy. I'll be fine," she said. That little girl was so wise. She was right. She was fine. I knew then that I would love Rose and Chuck forever.

In November of this year, my big sister Liz came down to see our mom. She also went to one of my treatments with me. When she saw what the radiation had done to my skin, she cringed and turned her head. On the ride home, we talked.

"Will your skin stay that dark?" she asked.

"I don't know," I responded. "I have to put aloe vera on it and let it air-dry. One of my nurses said it would help it heal faster. It doesn't matter because they just keep putting that radiation on it. Madea said it's like lying in the sun all day, burning."

The rest of the ride home was quiet. While Liz was here, my mom called a meeting with me, Liz, and my sister Yolanda. She told us that in the event of her demise, she wanted us to handle the funeral plans. This type of conversation was not what I wanted to hear. History has shown that our family meetings were never filled with good news. But we told our mom we would take care of everything.

I slept a lot during my treatment journey. I wasn't very hungry while going through treatment. It made me very tired. I slept more than I ate. I found myself sleeping twelve hours a day. I missed much of the kids' school days. As I approached my last days of treatment, I loaned Chuck and Rose my coloring book to take home. Chuck wanted to color something as a token of our friendship. It was so cute. It was two bloodhounds. He said it was him and me. When I got home, I framed it and hung it on the bedroom wall. Rose, Chuck, and I made a pact that we would keep in touch as long as we could. They were both retired and said we could stop by anytime. Chuck and I talked on the phone at least once a week. Two times if one of us had an appointment.

Now my D cup was back to a C. Actually it was now a C minus. I was getting back to some of my routine. I had to take it easy because the side effects of radiation would last at least three more months. I found myself sleeping a lot still. My appetite came back and I wanted everything! For weeks, I slept and ate as much as I could. My hair began to fall out and get thinner. I gained weight, and I felt like I was losing control. The doctors didn't tell me to expect this. I was depressed because of my hair loss and weight gain. Yes, it's vain but who cares! Plus I couldn't do the marathon this coming year because I had to let my breast area heal. I tried to snap out of it but nothing was working. Walking up a small flight of stairs was too much for me to bear. I would get winded and have to stop halfway.

Two months later, a light bulb went off in my head. I realized I couldn't just lie down anymore. I couldn't let cancer win. I was lying in bed, dreading the day's activities when my body just hopped up. I got dressed, brushed my teeth, and went outside. The sun felt good on my face. I smiled toward it with my eyes closed. This was what I needed—I needed to feel the sun and the Son. It's not that I couldn't feel God in my room but it was dark and gloomy, and I had to get out of that dark place in order to see Him.

I went back to school that semester. I was ready! I was energized! I called the youth minister at my church and told him I wanted to go back to working with the youth. He told me to slow down and not to get back into things too quickly. Of course I didn't listen to him. I was back in full swing the next week. I was to graduate from junior college in the spring. I called my mom and told her I would be graduating and she was happy for me. It was God's grace and mercy that allowed me to be able to get up and get busy working in the kingdom again. I didn't want to waste any more time. Spring brought about change. I had to make up the classes I dropped when I was first diagnosed. I was still excited though. However, I still didn't know how sick Madea was.

CROSS-YOUR-HEART BRA

*These bras had a cross design and are seamless
to create a soft cup and smooth flattering look.*

The new spring semester was approaching. My grandmother passed away the previous year, leaving all of us hurting and a little uncertain about a few things like leadership in the Washington lineage. I missed her dearly. I continued saying the Lord's Prayer at bedtime and sometimes during the day when things were tough. I was deep in thought when our phone rang and my husband answered it.

"May I speak to Laura?" the voice asked.

"May I ask who's calling?" my husband replied.

"My name is Ricky. Ricky Jones. We've been friends since fifth grade."

"It's someone named Ricky Jones," my husband said.

"*What*!" I replied. "I ain't heard from that boy since I was in high school."

"Do you want to speak with him?" he asked me.

"Yes," I said. "Hi, Ricky! How are you?"

"I'm good," he said with a shaky voice.

"Hello?" I asked.

"I'm here," he responded. "I just thought I would never hear your voice again. I've never stopped loving you, Laura."

"Hey!" I said reluctantly. "After I left Georgia and came back to California I was very busy with school and junior college. How did you get my number?" I knew Granny was gone and she was his main connection.

"I called your uncle in Georgia and he gave me your number."

"Oh, really?"

We exchanged pleasantries, asked about each other's parents and such. He now has a daughter. Her name is Linda.

"Why Linda?" I asked.

"I wanted to name her Laura but my girlfriend heard about you and said no."

I laughed so loud I thought I would throw up. He still loved me. It was an awkward but sweet conversation.

"Who was the man who answered the phone?" he asked.

"That was my husband."

"You're married?" he asked.

"Yes! For over four years now," I responded.

"I thought you would wait for me?" he said. "You crossed your heart and promised."

"Ricky, that was when we were kids. We hadn't been in touch for years and things have changed. How's your mom?" I asked as a way of changing the subject.

"She's fine. Getting older and on my nerves. She loves her granddaughter. She reminds me of you. Things haven't changed for me. I wish you would have waited," he stated.

I was very puzzled to know she acted like me considering I wasn't her mother. Nor was I related to his girlfriend's family. I told Ricky how Dee-Dee passed away some years ago and how my granny passed away the year before, and I told him of my diagnosis with all the gory details.

"I can come take care of you if you need me to," he said.

"I'm okay. I'll be okay. God's got me," I replied. "It was good to hear from you but I need to get off the phone. I am very tired." Truth was, I didn't know what else to say to him.

"It was good hearing your voice," he said.

"You too," I replied.

"I love you," he said.

"Take care, Ricky." What was I supposed to say? I wasn't going to say it back. He was holding on to something and hoping for something I couldn't give him.

It was a rough winter season, both academically and emotionally. Mom's health was fading, I was still fighting off the effects of radiation therapy while also digging myself out of a depressive state, and my marriage was in an uncertain place. I felt I wasn't getting enough support from my spouse with the kids while feeling tired all the time, and he was tired from work as well.

I went over to my mother's house to visit. I took my daughter with me. Mom and Dad always had goodies stashed away somewhere and I needed a break. I also missed her. I had been away from her for a while during treatment. My oncologist said I needed to rest, stay out of the sun, and be careful of germs. Unnecessary trips outside of the home were not allowed. Dad opened the door for me. Mom was resting in the room. Dad and I talked for a while, and I heard my mother call my name.

"Laura?" she called.

"Ma'am?" I responded. See, even though I was a California girl, those few years spent in the South changed the way I respond to adults though I was one.

"Bring me some water please!"

I took a glass of water to her. She and Dad were now sleeping in separate rooms because Mom would get sick at night from her chemo treatments and didn't want to disturb his sleep. When I entered her room, she was sitting on the edge of the bed, going through papers. I gave her the updates on our favorite soap operas and the goings on at church. Usually she's very interested but she didn't seem to care at this time. Whenever my mom, grandmother, and aunts were cleaning and throwing out things, it usually meant visitors were coming.

"Either someone is coming or going. Which is it?" I asked.

"How are the kids?" she asked deflecting my question.

I went on to tell her how the boys were. My daughter saw that my mom was still in her pajamas.

"Why are you in your pajamas, Bamms?" she asked.

"I don't feel too good today, baby," Mom replied.

"Why?" my daughter asked.

"I have an owie, baby," she replied.

"Can I pray for you?" Mara asked.

My mom was shocked but said yes. My daughter walked over to my mom, closed her eyes, and began to pray. Neither of us could hear anything she said, but when I looked up, her lips were moving. This child knew enough to pray for her grandmother when she was ill.

"Amen!" my daughter said.

"Amen!" both my mom and I answered.

We hung around for a little while and my mom continued throwing things away and cleaning out drawers.

"Here! You can have this," she said.

It was the ring my sister Dee-Dee once wore. It was the ring she was killed for.

"Why are you giving me this?" I asked.

My mother didn't respond to my question.

"Is everything okay, Momma? Are you going somewhere?" I asked.

"Somewhere," she replied.

My daughter and I gave my mom kisses, told my Dad goodbye, then we left. I was wondering what she meant by the "somewhere" comment but was too tired to investigate it. Looking back, I wish I had the courage to ask my mom more questions without being afraid. I could have been more of a support. In my naivete, I really didn't want to know the truth. My mother was sick and dying and I was selfish, too selfish to ask for the truth.

I also thought back to when I was diagnosed the first time and kept so much from my kids because my husband and I thought they were too young to understand. Though me and my mother were close, a small disconnect came when she got sick the first time. I was afraid then and now to ask the deeper questions. And perhaps Madea thought I was still too young to understand as well. Or maybe she didn't want me to think my fate would turn out the same as hers. I'll never know because I didn't ask.

PADDED BRAS

Young women and seasoned women alike wear padded bras. This is to give the illusion of having more than what is actually there.

Rose, Chuck, and I had lunch a few times as time progressed. Our conversations usually centered on our diagnosis, prognosis, our blood counts, and my daughter. Rose seemed to be bored. Our conversations were like a foreign language to her. She adored my daughter and was always excited to hear about her. Chuck told me of how he's now wearing netted underpants. This is to keep the area cool while he's going through radiation. Though Chuck was in his early seventies, he was very concerned about proper function in that area. My heart melted for him because when he spoke, he would turn red in the face with embarrassment but his eyes were full of desperation. Rose assured him that she loved him as he was, and at their age, that's not a big concern. I could only try and imagine what a man must have to deal with psychologically and emotionally when going through radiation treatment for such a delicate area.

I went home and shared my visit to my mom's with my husband and he thought the same as I—that someone was coming to visit because his mother did the same things when visitors came. The rest of our day was simple with me sleeping and the kids playing throughout the house. I was resting in my room when I heard the phone ring.

"Hello?" I answered.

"Laura?" Madea said.

"Yes, ma'am?" I replied.

"I need you to take me to the doctor in a couple days."

"Um. Okay," I answered. "Are we going to the same local hospital?"

"No. I need to go see my oncologist."

"Okay, Madea. I'll take you."

"Thank you. Robert will be here when you come and he'll open the door for you."

"Okay. See you then."

My mom hung up the phone and I sat up in bed, wondering what that conversation was all about. I guess you can say I was very close-minded during this season about my mother's health. She did not share much and I didn't ask much either. The main reason was that I didn't want to know because I was scared. I rolled over and prayed for my mom that everything would be all right and that she was just dealing with a cold.

When I entered the house, I hugged my dad.

"She's in her room in the back," Dad said.

"Thanks, Dad," I said.

Walking to her room seemed to take a very long time. Maybe it was my hesitation coupled with anxiety. Mom was in the bathroom. When I came around the corner from the hallway, I saw she was standing in front of the mirror. She looked very weak and frail.

"Mom?" I asked. "What's wrong?"

"I need help getting dressed," she said.

At that moment, I knew something was very wrong with her. My mother was the type of woman who rarely asked for help doing anything. Even if it took her a week to get something done, she wouldn't ask for assistance, especially with putting on her undergarments. I gladly stepped to her to help her get dressed. I did her hair, helped her brush her teeth, put lotion on her body, put her bra on her, made her sit down so I could put her pants on her, her blouse, socks, shoes, and her jacket.

"Daddy? We're ready to go!" I shouted.

"Okay," he said firmly.

Dad helped me walk Mom to the car. After we got her in, I was sure to drive slowly in case she was feeling nauseous.

"Why are you driving so slow?" she asked.

"I want to make sure you're comfortable."

"Baby, please drive faster. I don't feel well," Madea said.

And from then on, my speed was over the limit. Now maybe people will understand why I drive so fast. When we arrived at the hospital, Mom told me to get her a wheelchair. I frowned at the request but did as I was told. I pushed her to the location of her doctor's office. They immediately took her in. They were expecting her. While Madea was away, I wandered the halls, looking at colorful art done by previous patients. Many of these patients were children of various ages. One of them was as young as three years old. I winced at the thought. Still unsure of what was going on, I asked the receptionist for an update.

"They are giving your mother some blood through a transfusion because she's too weak."

"Weak? Blood? I don't understand," I said. "Where is her doctor?"

"I'll get him, honey. Hold on," she said.

As long as I can remember, my family has been secretive about things such as illnesses, money, and relationships. In turn, we grew up following the same pattern set before us. I vowed I would not do that to my children but I did. Then, I heard a voice call out.

"The family of Eloise Johnson?" someone said.

"Here I am!" I replied.

"Hi. I'm told you have some questions," the doctor said.

"Yes," I said firmly. "Why is my mom so weak and why does she need blood?"

"Your mother's blood count is low, and when that happens, we have to do a transfusion so she can feel strong."

"But I don't understand. What is happening that's making her so weak?" With hesitancy, the doctor gave me a response.

"Your mother's cancer has returned in the uterus and it's spreading quickly. She's been coming here now for almost a year for chemotherapy. Didn't she or your father tell you?"

"No, sir!" I responded with a shaky voice. "They didn't."

"She's very strong but the cancer is moving so fast that she can't keep up. This is why she comes here for blood. I have to get back now. I think you should speak with your parents so they can give you more information. I'm sorry I don't have better news."

"Thank you, doctor."

The doctor left me standing in the middle of the room, alone. My head hurt and nothing was making sense. An hour later, my mother was brought out. She was done for the day. As I wheeled her back to the car, I had so many questions but wasn't sure how to ask or where to begin. The drive home was quiet. I played the Christian talk radio station as a way of providing a peaceful ride. When I worked with my mom and we rode together, we always listened to this station going to and from work. Eventually I grew to enjoy it. I was deep in thought when I heard my mom's voice.

"Laura? Could you stop at the store and get me a 7 Up?" she asked.

"Yes, ma'am," I said.

I stopped at the store closest to her house so she wouldn't have to wait in the car too long. When we arrived at the house, my dad was watering the grass in the front yard.

"How'd it go?" he asked.

No one answered his question. I just gave him a look of concern. I helped Madea back to her room, tucked her in, and then I got up the nerve to ask.

"Mom. What's wrong with you?"

"I have cancer," she replied.

"Really? Why?"

I know that seemed like a dumb question at the time but I was in little-girl-asking-my-mommy-a-serious-question mode.

"Well, it came back. This time, with a vengeance," she said.

"Can they get rid of it?" I asked.

"They've been trying to do that now for a year but all it's doing is slowing it down."

We sat in silence for about twenty minutes until it was broken by my dad's voice.

"Eloise, you hungry?"

"No, Robert. I'm fine. Thank you," she responded.

"You hungry, Laura?"

"Yes, sir!" I replied.

"The food will be on the table in fifteen minutes. Wash your hands and come on in," he said.

"Go on," my mom said and she shooed me away.

When I entered the dining room, he had a full setup just for us. My dad always had a way of making me feel like a special guest when I came over for any meal. He would have all the place settings with napkins, silverware, and all other supplies needed so I wouldn't have to get up from the table. Plus I think it bothered him to get up once he sat down. My grandmother was the same way. Whatever didn't make it to the table probably wasn't necessary.

"Daddy. What's wrong with her?" I asked in my little-girl voice.

"I'm not sure your mother wants you to know everything. Did you ask her?"

"Yes, sir. I did."

"What did she say?" he asked.

"She said her cancer was back and it was worse this time."

"Did she tell you anything else?"

"No, sir. She didn't."

"Well, so be it. That's the way she wants it. Let's bless the food and eat."

"Daddy, I need more time. I need more cushion."

"Father God, bless this food we are about to receive. Bless the hands that prepared it. Sanctify it for the nourishing of our bodies. In Your name, we pray. Amen."

While my daddy was praying, I was praying and crying. As old as I was, I still felt like a little girl when I was around the two of them but especially in this moment. My mother had always portrayed herself as self-sufficient, strong, healthy, and full of life when we were around. But now, she was sick, weak, and couldn't help herself. My father was being vague about her prognosis and I didn't know who to ask for more information. On the way home, I decided to call my big sister Liz. As it turned out, she didn't know much either. Or at least, that's what she told me. After the visit with my mom, a lot of my days went by quickly. So much is a blur. I was still feeling the effects of the radiation treatment. My kids were busy with school, my husband had work, and I was preparing to start school in the fall season. But first, I had to get through summer. I was excited to get back to school. I enjoyed learning and I was scheduled to graduate the following year in May. The first person I called about graduation was my mom.

"Mom. Guess what?"

"Baby, I don't feel like guessing. Tell me what it is," Mom sounded so weak and I didn't pick up on what she was trying to tell me.

"I'll be graduating in May 2002," I told her.

"That's good, baby. I'm proud of you."

"Thanks. Since I lost a semester because of treatment, it set me back but one more year won't make a big difference."

"Glad you're finishing up, baby," she said. "I'll call you later. Bye."

"Bye, Momma."

After I hung up the phone, I went to call my husband and let him know. We had been planning a five-year-anniversary party. With my health changes and our marriage taking on an additional strain for various reasons, we needed something to celebrate. I was considered to be in remission in my mind, but medically, a patient was not considered in remission until they go five years without a recurrence. Again I was deep in thought when my phone rang again. It was my mom.

"Laura, I got your invitation to the party but I can't remember the date. When is it?" she asked.

"July 6. It's on a Saturday so you and Dad can come."

"Hmmm. Okay. Thanks," Madea said. She hung up the phone.

I completed my radiation treatments and I had to be examined thoroughly for the next five years. I had oncology appointments every six months, mammograms yearly, Pap smear exams every six months, MRIs yearly, and ultrasounds with a chemical dye placed in my body to see my bones and if any cancer was present. This took a toll on me emotionally and psychologically. Though I believed I was healed in Jesus's name, I still had anxiety facing the radiologist each year. I gained so much weight and was feeling unworthy. My thoughts of when I was a child came rushing back. I had opted for a lumpectomy because I didn't want to lose my breast. I felt I wasn't a complete woman without both of them. The assurance I needed was not there as I had hoped. I thought back to when Ricky loved me for me but we were children. We didn't know about real love or real-life challenges.

I continued planning our anniversary party. In between time, I visited my Mom and Dad. I had no idea this would be the last time I would speak to her in her home, in her bed.

Chapter 10

STRAPLESS BRAS

The purpose of the strapless bra is to enable women to wear dresses or tops that do not have sleeves or straps. Depending on circumstances and movement, it may not work well.

My big sister Liz was in town to check on Madea. She was sleeping a lot and not talking very much. I went over to see her as well, but this time, I had the kids with me. I told them to stay in the living room while I went into her room to speak with her.

"How you feeling, Mom?" I asked.

"My head hurts, baby," she said softly.

"Do you want me to get you something?" I asked.

"No. I'll be okay," she replied.

As I have done most of my life when I wasn't feeling well, or my mom was ill, I lay down next to her to feel her body. I placed my hand gently on her head and began to pray silently. I was praying for her healing and for her not to die. My mom must have sensed what I was praying for and pulled away as if to stop me from putting in my request to God. Still I was not aware of what was going on. I left the room and went into the living room where the kids were.

"Is Bamms okay?" Mara asked.
"She's tired, sweetie. Let's say a prayer for her, okay?"
"Okay, Mommy," she said.
"Mom. Is Bamms gonna be okay?" Jonathan asked.
"I hope so, son," I replied.

The next day, my mom was moved to the hospital for observation. I went to see her. My two older sisters were there as well as my brother-in-law and Uncle David. It was my turn to go in and see her. I was very nervous. Her last hospital trip went through my head but I was determined to go in and see her this time.

"Hi, Momma," I said.
"Hi, baby," she said softly.

She reached out her hand to me as if to call me to her side. I sat next to her. She rubbed my hand and rested her eyes for a bit. Her skin was dark and clammy. It was a beautiful day outside. I opened her blinds but she squinted her eyes as if the light bothered her. Her oncologist entered the room and gave her some information that I was not listening to. I followed him out to the hallway.

"Doctor, what's wrong with my mom?" I asked.

"Your mother's cancer is very advanced. There is nothing more we can do for her now. We are going to place her on hospice where they'll keep her comfortable. She will be transported later this evening," he said.

"How long does she have?" I asked.

"It could be anywhere from three weeks to three months," he said assuredly.

You would think at my age, I understood the gravity of what he was saying but I didn't. I went to the waiting room with the rest of the family and talked for a bit. Then I left to pick up my kids from my in-laws. I told my husband of the new information. I also went to see Pastor M to give him an update.

"Be there as much as you can while you can and love her as much as you can while you can. It's in God's hands," he said. With tears in my eyes, I left his office. This just didn't make sense to me.

I was still planning our five-year-anniversary party and she was supposed to be there. I had new furniture being delivered the next day as well as a cleaning team coming to the house and I wanted to be sure everything was in good condition and cleaned properly. Mom was transported the next day, Friday, and when I was done with my errands, I went to see her. By now, many of my siblings, cousins, nieces, and nephews were in town. The hospice care facility was down the street from me so we could go see her as often as we wanted. I walked into the facility and saw many nurses and visitors for other patients. When I walked into my mom's room, one of my uncles was with her.

"Hey there, sweetie," he said.

"Hi, Uncle," I said. I gave him a hug. My uncle left so we could talk.

"Where are the kids?" Madea asked.

"Hi, sunshine! They're at the house with their dad," I answered.

I gave her a kiss on the lips. Her voice sounded soft and raspy but clear. She didn't appear to be in any pain and was a bit upbeat. Her eyes were closed most of the time. I assumed it was because the light bothered her. Daddy was on the patio, sitting and talking with one of my uncles. My aunt was in the foyer, talking with other visitors. One of the nurses came in to check on her.

"Nurse?" I called out. "When will she get something to eat?" I asked.

"Let me check on that for you," she responded. About two minutes later, the head nurse came in.

"Did someone have a question?" she asked.

"Yes. I did. When will my mother get to eat?"

"We don't administer any meals here. We basically keep her comfortable."

"I don't understand. Why wouldn't you feed her?" It was clear to the head nurse that I had no clue as to what hospice care meant. The head nurse left the room. Later I found out my mom's cancer was very advanced; the doctor's estimate was more like a cushion because no one but God really knows. Mom's cancer had returned and it had now spread to her brain through her spine. This is why she had headaches and the light bothered her. It was only a matter of time now, but still, my dad and I were clueless. I turned to my mom to see if she needed anything.

"Are you thirsty?" I asked.

"No. I'm fine," she replied.

"Okay. I have to leave now and get the kids, and I have a meeting tonight to prepare for Youth Day," I told her.

"Okay, baby," she said. "I love you," Mom said.

"I love you too, sunshine," I said.

Her eyes were open now. I kissed my mom on the lips again and on the head.

"See you tomorrow," I told her.

"Uh-huh," she said.

I looked back at her as I left her room. She lifted her hand to wave to me and I smiled. The next day, Saturday, I went in to see Mom and she didn't look the same. Her body was jerking often and she was making noises. I was told that her body was fighting against dying and this was normal. She could no longer hear me. Our conversations were over. I didn't want to see her this way anymore so I left and went home. Again, I was running away.

The next day, Sunday, I went to see her after church. Her body was now very calm. Her breathing was labored but I was told she could hear me. She was no longer moving but very, very still, resting; but her heart was still beating. I climbed into the bed with her. I lay down on her right side, put my arm around her, grabbed her hand, buried my head in her neck, and cried. I don't know how long I cried but it was so long, and I shed so many tears that it soaked the top part of her gown. I fell asleep. I was awakened by the nurse coming in to check her heartbeat.

"It's very faint but steady," the nurse said. She left with her head bowed down.

I slipped out of the bed to go see my dad and my aunt. I hugged them tightly.

"You okay?" my aunt asked.

"I'm okay, Auntie," I replied.

I went home to check on the kids and get something to eat. It was too late in the day to go see my mom. I went upstairs and cried myself to sleep. The next morning, Monday, July 1, at 8:01 a.m., I received a call from my mother's older brother.

"Hello?" I said in a soft voice.

"Laura. Your momma is gone," he said.

"Huh?" I asked in shock.

"She's gone, baby. She's in the arms of the Lord now," he said.

"Okay. Thank you," I said with a shaky voice. I called Pastor M to let him know. He prayed with me over the phone.

"Let me know if you need anything," he said.

"I will. Thank you."

I called my husband at work to inform him Madea died. My brain was in a fog. He said he'd pick up the kids from school and take them to his mom's house and bring them home later that evening. After I got off the phone with him, I went to the hospice facility to see my mom. When I arrived, there were quite a few people there from our family. I walked into her room and her little body was very still. It was too quiet. I saw my dad sitting on the patio outside her room. I climbed in the bed with her again and cried like a baby. My brother Vincent, the one I call my twin, knelt on the floor, next to her bedside, and cried with me. I could hear my uncle telling me to get up so they could take her body but I didn't want to leave her. Twenty minutes later, we were still lying there. For those who do not know, when a loved one dies in hospice care, the family is given ample time to stay with the decedent. They say the time can be as long as you need, but honestly, it isn't. I know this because I never wanted them to take her body away.

I went out on the patio with my dad and we cried together. About ten minutes later, the porters entered the room to take my mom's body to the morgue. They took her out through the patio entrance of her room and drove off. Immediately I began to work with my dad to get arrangements completed. Liz had gone back to Atlanta a few days prior and was making plans to return for the funeral. My family was very supportive with planning. I took clothing, makeup, and jewelry to the funeral home. I told the family services coordinator that my mother didn't wear much makeup and to please not make her look like a stripper. A couple days later, my sister-in-law, Gloria, and I went to the funeral home to be sure her body was presentable for a viewing. It was. They did a wonderful job. She looked peaceful and happy. She wore the white suit I once wore for a special occasion. I sang at my mom's funeral, and when it was time for us to have our final view, I gripped the side of the casket so hard I heard it crack. I kissed her forehead and walked away. I was hurting. The circumstances and activities I was facing made me feel like I was falling and I needed support, support only God could give me. Though I know death is part of life, I thought my mother would live forever.

We buried my mother on my fifth wedding anniversary and our party was scheduled the next day. All the guests who were invited, 150 to be exact, showed up. I believe my mother made a deal with God to allow her to pass during the week of the party so my brothers and sisters could attend. This was the first time we'd been together since my sister Dee-Dee passed away in 1987. I was able to take a photo with all of my siblings and my dad. Though I missed her dearly, I love my mother even more now because she orchestrated one of the best parties I'd had in a long time. Family from the East Coast, Southern California, and Texas were in town and they celebrated her life and us. I needed this. My marriage and our children needed this. Thanks, Madea.

CUT AND PASTE: MY NINTH-HOUR EXPERIENCE

In the years that followed, I took another semester off from school. I missed my mother's presence and trying to concentrate on my studies was difficult. My kids were missing her too. I had gotten back into running marathons and helping out at my church. The first few months were tough physically but I managed well.

I graduated from junior college in the month of May 2005. I cried for most of the day because I missed my mom. Though she had already said she was proud of me, I needed her there. I was holding down a part-time job as a facilitator, teaching family communication classes while still being a full-time wife and mother. I continued my appointments as instructed by my ob-gyn and oncologist. I took my medications daily. It had been four years since my diagnosis and I couldn't wait until I hit my five-year mark to be declared officially in remission.

Many people may or may not understand how much of a strain a cancer diagnosis places on a family, especially a young active family as my own. My children's schedules were nonstop. My sixteen and seventeen-year-olds sang in the youth choir at church and played basketball. The twins were in fifth grade and very active in the choir at church and with basketball and track. My daughter was in second grade and was also very active in the children's choir at church, Praise Dance, and other afterschool activities. I was back to my normal grind. I was wearing a filler bra but was still energetic about my activities at home, my kids' school, work, and church. My last follow-up appointments were scheduled for October and November 2006. My October appointment went well. My white blood cell count was a little low, but that was because I was doing too much and not resting enough. My oncologist wasn't too concerned but said that I should take more time to rest completely. I told him I would.

In November, I had my last mammogram before going to the yearly checkups. As usual, I was nervous and anxious about going in but had the attitude of a conqueror. The technician who conducted my exam was the same woman from 2001 with my first diagnosis. She remembered me. It's not unusual to talk about odd things during a mammogram. It's awkward enough being handled and your breasts placed on the plastic microwave dish. She was understanding this time as she'd been before. She told me to sit in the waiting room but not to take off my gown in case she needed more films. I did as instructed and waited.

"Laura Franklin." I heard my name called.

"Yes?" I answered.

"Take these to the radiology department," she said with a gloomy look on her face. I already knew what that meant. I had been here before. That long walk down the hall to radiology was all too familiar. I went into the undressing room and shed a few tears. I got dressed and walked briskly to the other building. I hid my face behind the film's case so no one would see my tears. As I approached the radiology department, I called my husband to let him know what happened. I hung up the phone and went inside. I gave the films to the receptionist and waited to be called. I prayed while I waited.

"Laura Franklin!" someone called out.

I got up and followed the employee who called my name. I was directed to the same room as before, almost five years prior. The doctor who conducted my first biopsy was there. This was the worst déjà vu in the world.

"Sit down, Mrs. Franklin," she said. "I won't try and sugarcoat this. You've been here before. We found more calcium clusters in your left breast but in a different area. We know from your previous films that they weren't there before."

As she spoke, tears ran down my face but I never broke my stare at her and I was listening more intently than before. I was wearing a white blouse. I cried so many tears that one could see through the blouse. As she continued talking, my current oncologist walked past the office and saw me crying.

"What's wrong?" he asked.

"My cancer is back!" I said in a shaky voice.

"We got through it the first time and we'll do it again. I'll be right there with you," he said and bowed his head. He squeezed my arm and spoke to the radiologist about the diagnosis.

"Keep me updated on her please," he said.

"I will, doctor," she replied.

I wiped my face, told the biopsy doctor thank you. I was told I would receive a call from someone in the surgery department. On November 14, 2006, I was diagnosed once again with DCIS. I didn't have to meet with any of the specialist as I did for the first diagnosis but I did meet with the same surgeon.

"I'm sorry about the recurrence, Mrs. Franklin," he said.

"Thank you, doctor. Me too," I replied.

"As you know, you have many options. You can do a double mastectomy, partial mastectomy with reconstruction, or another lumpectomy. We are going to get you connected with another surgeon in our Los Angeles hospital for preparation. Take some time to think about which option you would like to choose. If you have any questions, call my office."

"Are you going to do the surgery again?" I asked.

"Yes. I will," he replied.

This made me happy. He handed me a form with the number to the Los Angeles hospital in case I had questions. I left his office and headed to my car. The closer I got to the main door leading out-

I STUFF MY BRA... *SO WHAT?*

side, the more the tears flowed. I couldn't hold them in any longer. As soon as I got outside, I stopped by the big fountain and cried my tears there. My face was in my hands.

One of the good things about crying at a hospital is no one bothers you. I paused a moment to call my husband. He asked me to stop by his job which was a few miles away. When I got there, he came outside to see me. He gave me a hug.

"What do you want to do?" he asked.

"I'm not sure," I answered. Feeling, once again, irritated with his questions since history was repeating itself and remembering the lack of support with the first diagnosis, I was intentionally short with my responses. "The doctor gave me many options. I have a lot to think about."

"Do you want me to come home?" he asked.

"No," I replied indifferently. "I'm gonna go by the church to tell Pastor and make preparations for surgery. They will call me with a date and time."

"Okay," he said. "Call me if you need anything."

"I will," I answered. Then I left.

As I headed to the church, I thought of my babies and the teens I teach during the week. This feeling was different because the Lord showed me why it returned and this gave me pause. A behavior and thought process of mine had continued. Though me and the Lord were connected, I wasn't as close to Him as I should have been. The cancer was back and I didn't know how much I would have to endure. I entered the church foyer and knocked on the pastor's office door.

"Come in," he said.

When I entered, he saw my red eyes.

"What's wrong?" he said.

I sat down, took a deep breath, and gave him the news.

"My cancer is back. It's in the same breast but a different part," I said.

"Let's pray," he said.

As he prayed, more tears flowed. I wanted my mom but she was gone. I was angry because I needed her. We discussed coverage for the classes I was teaching and my other duties at church.

"Don't worry about any of that. Just take care of yourself," he said. "I'll be there!"

"Thank you for the prayers," I said.

I left his office and headed home. Later that night, I told my husband I wanted to be the one to tell the older boys. The last time this happened, they were much younger and didn't understand what was going on. They only knew I was sick. As I told my boys what was going on, they raised their hands with questions as if they were in school.

"Are you gonna die?" Jonathan asked.

"I don't think so," I replied. "Your Bamms once told me that all sickness is not unto death."

"Who's gonna take us to school?" Jedidiah asked.

"I will until I have surgery. After that, it'll be your dad or Aunt Liz," I answered.

I could see on their faces the sadness and fear of losing me to this disease. I had to stay strong for them. If I broke out in tears, they would as well. I didn't want them to see me cry.

"I need you guys to look out for the twins and your baby sister and do what you're told. I am not afraid. I already prayed and God has given me confirmation. He is with me."

I left out of their room and closed the door. I stood outside the room for a few minutes to hear what they were saying. They discussed me dying and what they would do without me. Then I heard them crying. I peeked in the room and saw them hugging each other. I knew then that my babies would be fine, no matter what happened. I prayed as I went upstairs to my room to rest.

This reminded me of when my mother was ill the last time and she didn't give the family a lot of information on her condition. Privacy was important to her but it also caused division between us. I wanted to be connected to my kids through this second trial. Though I didn't give them all the information they needed, they did know enough to pray for and love on each other.

I received a call from the Los Angeles hospital the next morning. I needed to meet with the surgeon to discuss more options. I went in a few days later. He wanted to do the surgery before Thanksgiving.

My prior doctor would not do the surgery due to the scheduling. This saddened me.

"I'm sorry, doctor. That does not work with my schedule. I have five young children and I need to prepare them and my household for my absence."

"How much time do you need?" he asked.

"I need a few weeks, at the least," I replied.

"We'll schedule you for December 12," he said.

"Great! The day after my birthday," I responded sarcastically.

In between preparing my household, my children, my family, and my church, I had to go to the Los Angeles office often. I had to give them my decision as to what option I chose. I decided to take photos of my chest area with my Polaroid camera. In the first picture, I covered my breast to get an idea of what it may look like without it and another one with both. I looked at both pictures, prayed, and made my decision. I was at peace with it all. I called my husband in the room to tell him.

"Hey. What's up?" he asked.

"I've made a decision on which surgery I will do," I said.

"What did you choose?" he asked.

"Well, with the lumpectomy, they'll just take out portions and I'll have to wear a new filler and possibly have more breast tissue scooped out again in the future."

"What's wrong with that?" he asked.

"Nothing I guess, but the possibility of it coming back a third time is too much to think about. I don't want to be a guinea pig the rest of my life. Does it matter to you which option I choose, if I have both breasts?" I asked him.

"Yes, it matters," he answered emphatically.

"Okay. Well, I chose to do the mastectomy with reconstruction."

I remember meeting a woman named Lisa. She'd been a visitor at my church a couple times. She was invited by one of the members she rides the train with into work. Lisa approached me after service and I found out she was also a cancer survivor. After sharing our concerns and my fear of having the surgery, Lisa did something crazy!

"You'll enjoy the reconstruction," she said with enthusiasm.

"Excuse me?" I replied.

"You wanna see something?" she asked while grabbing her right breast.

"See what?" I asked. My facial expression informed her that I was clearly confused at her proposal.

"Where's the restroom?" Lisa asked. I led her out of the sanctuary and into the hallway to the women's restroom. "I wanna show you something," she said.

"It's right here. Why?" I asked. Laughing out loud, Lisa grabbed my hand and led me inside.

She checked all the stalls to see if anyone else was there. Once she realized it was clear, she raised her blouse to flash me.

"Look!" she said.

"Whoa! I don't git down like that?" I explained. Laughing at me again, Lisa explained herself.

"I don't either. This is my reconstructed breast. Wanna feel it?"

"Nope! I'm good." Still feeling uncomfortable but intrigued at the look of it. "What is that?"

"It's silicone. I couldn't do the reconstruction with belly fat or muscle from my lats so they did implants. I'm going to have the other one done so they match in size and shape," Lisa said.

"Wow! That's crazy!"

"You wanna touch it?" she asked. Reluctantly I did. It was eerie.

"Does it hurt?" I asked.

"No. But the thing with silicone is I may have to have it replaced in ten years or sooner if they leak. So see, reconstruction isn't all that bad. I still have treatment for another two months and then I can do the new surgery." Lisa and I stayed in the bathroom and cried a little and hugged a lot. I thanked her for sharing with me. She has a five-year-old daughter who has watched her go through this ordeal. She is unsure if her daughter has the BRCA gene and will test her when her daughter is ten years old. Lisa and I finally came out of the restroom. My husband was waiting for me.

"What happened? Where were you?" he asked.

I STUFF MY BRA... *SO WHAT?*

"I had to talk to a lady about breast cancer and reconstruction surgery. She confirmed some things for me and gave me some really great advice and insight."

"Are you still going to do the mastectomy?" he asked.

"Yes! For sure!" his face changed immediately due to disappointment. The drive home was very quiet between us. The only noise came from the kids in the back seat.

Okay now, back to my conversation with my husband. Let me explain something before y'all go karate chop him for his response. Men are visual creatures as we all know. My husband couldn't see the beauty in the surgery. He wasn't looking at me through God's eyes but through his own. Though it hurt to hear what he said and it made me feel less than whole—and yes, I told my big sister and a few others—I moved on because my health was at stake. What I did not tell you is, before I told my husband of my decision, I made sure to consult with the Lord. I ran upstairs to pray. Before I prayed, I lay down on my back on my bed. I was looking out the window and the trees were swaying and the birds chirping. I closed my eyes and began to pray. The birds stopped singing and the trees stopped swaying. The kids were automatically quiet downstairs. All outside distractions had ceased. As I prayed, I apologized to God for not coming to Him sooner. In my spirit, I asked, *What do you want me to do, Lord?*

"Trust me," He said.

"I can do that," I replied.

I began to cry and say, "Thank you, Jesus," over and over until I fell asleep. I slept for three hours.

During the next appointment, I told the surgeon of my decision. He explained to me the entire procedure and that I was a good candidate for it. The surgery would take four hours, including the reconstruction. He used a black Sharpie to draw lines around the area to be cut. He took pictures of me facing front and with my back to him. I watched videos and testimonials on breast reconstruction. While sitting in the video room alone, I was overwhelmed at the photos of the before and after of each woman. None of the women in the videos were African American and they seemed to be old enough to be my mother. I cried while watching the second video because I saw the scars on their chest area, sides near the rib cage, and lower abdomens. To me, it looked like they were a cut-and-paste art project. I was alone and horrified! I wanted to leave. Ten minutes after the videos were complete, one of the female coordinators walked in.

"You ready, Mrs. Franklin?" she asked.

"No! But does it matter?" I replied.

The appointment was three hours long. I was given a short tour to show me where I would go on the day of surgery and where my family would be waiting. After signing all the paperwork and receiving more instructions, I went home. I was mentally exhausted. My sister Liz would be flying in from Atlanta to help take care of me, and two women from my church said they would come visit the night before to have prayer with me. As we were closing out my last youth Bible study class, our youth minister asked me to sit in the middle of the room. I did.

"Class, I would like for us to lay hands on Sis. Franklin and pray for her. She is getting ready to face a tough battle and we want her to come back to us fully healed."

All of the youth were gathered around me in the room. I was shocked.

"Let's pray," he said.

I know my eyes should have been closed but they weren't. I was looking around the circle; these babies, who I had known for years, who I prayed for many times, were now praying for me. My eyes welled up with tears and I could no longer see clearly. I heard them say amen, and when I looked up, they too had tears in their eyes. I received many hugs and kisses from them. They told me they loved me and they would come to visit when they could. Somehow they knew about the cancer's return. I definitely felt the prayers.

About a week before my surgery, I started to feel unsure again. I asked God to show me if this was the right thing to do and that I would be okay. On the Sunday before surgery, another woman named Stephanie, a member of my church, came to me to talk. We began walking and she explained how she'd been diagnosed back in the '80s when there wasn't so much technology, as there is now, or medical advances. Most of the conversation is foggy but she got my attention when she pulled me into the bathroom. *What is it with these bathrooms?* I thought to myself.

"I wanna show you something," she said.

"What's wrong?" I asked. Realizing that I was confused as to what she had been trying to explain to me, she made a comment.

"I don't think you understand what it is I'm offering you." Now my eyes were wide open. She was gonna flash me too. *Oh no!* I thought.

"I don't understand," I said, sounding concerned. Stephanie raised her blouse to show me her reconstructed breast.

"I just wanted to offer you some encouragement as you get ready. This was over thirty years ago when we didn't have nearly as much to work with in hospitals. You wanna touch it?"

"Does it hurt?" I asked.

"No. I forget it's not real most of the time." I touched it quickly because I was weirded out and shocked. "You'll be fine, Laura. God's got you. You can close your mouth now."

We prayed together and hugged for a long time. I thanked her for sharing with me and showing me proof. When we exited the bathroom, I was speechless. Mostly because I had been pulled into the women's bathroom in this church twice for two women to flash me unexpectedly. She was sent by God to do another show-and-tell. I walked to my car and muttered, "Thank you, Lord," and drove home feeling 100 percent confident about my decision.

The night before the surgery was my thirty-ninth birthday. I sat in my living room with two ladies from my church, my husband, and my kids. Liz was upstairs, asleep. Was it me or was the air thick in the room? Maybe a little of both. I'm sure we were all thinking the same things. The ladies stayed for a couple hours and one of them said she'd drive us to the hospital. Before they left, they prayed with my whole family. The kids went to bed and so did I. My thoughts were of random things. I wondered what I would look like after surgery. Would there be food when I was done? Did I pack everything I needed? So much was on my mind and nothing at all. I wished my mom was here. My dad called me.

"Hello?" I answered.

"Laura? You okay?" he asked.
"I'm fine, Daddy. You okay?"
"Yeah. Just wanted to say take care and I love you."
"I love you too, Daddy. Good night."
"Night."

I don't remember falling asleep but I guess I did because the next thing I remember is the alarm going off. I got up, brushed my teeth, got dressed, and took one more look in the mirror before I left. I was told not to wear deodorant or lotions and no jewelry of any kind. I took my coloring book and crayons with me as I had before. I also brought my cell phone and my favorite soundtracks to play in the car on the drive. Donna Turner drove us in her Cadillac CTS. The ride was very smooth.

When we arrived, I was taken to the prep room and my family was to stay behind to wait for me. Initially they took my coloring book and crayons away but gave them back to me once I was in my gown. My sister Liz was the first to come in before surgery.

"I love you," she said. I could see she also wished Madea was here.

"I love you too," I responded.

After she left, my husband came in.

"How do you feel?" he asked.

"I don't really know. I wish my mom was here. I'm hungry."

"Well, you can't eat before surgery, you know that," he said jokingly.

"I know."

The nurses and anesthesiologist came in for some last-minute checks. They confirmed my name, the type of surgery I was scheduled for, and my next of kin to call in case of emergency. All boxes were checked. The crew told me once I get inside, I would slide onto another gurney. I was reminded that I would have a mask placed on my face and be told to count backward from one hundred. I nodded in agreement. It was time for them to take me in. I gave my coloring book and crayons to my husband, gave him a kiss, then they wheeled me away. I remember looking at the ceiling and thinking, *This building is very old.*

I STUFF MY BRA... *SO WHAT?*

With every surgery in my past, I always made it a point to look at the things around me. When I entered the operating room, I looked around. And to my horror, I saw the same type of caulking gun I had seen five years ago during my biopsy. I hoped they weren't going to use that again. The room had nine people in it. I felt kind of special to have so much attention.

"Hi, everyone!" I said.

"Hello!" they responded collectively.

"All right, Laura. I need you to scoot over for me to your right," one nurse said.

As I began to scoot over, I felt a little queasy. My stomach was empty.

"I feel sick, guys," I told them.

"Let's pause for a minute in case she throws up. It may be because of her nerves or empty stomach," the anesthesiologist stated.

After a few minutes, the nausea went away and we were back in business.

"Start counting backward, Laura, starting with one hundred," someone said.

"One hundred, 99, 98, blah, blah, blah." As I remember.

"She's out, guys! Let's go to work," I heard someone say.

The next things I remember were beeping noises and a lot of pain. My face hurt and so did my shoulders. A nurse was checking my vitals.

"Can you hear me, Laura?" she asked.

"Yes," I replied. She said some medical jargon I could not understand. The nurse left and then I could hear footsteps coming toward me. It was someone wearing heeled shoes. As the sound got closer, I knew who it was. It was Pastor M and his wife. He did not like hospitals but they came to see me.

"You're gonna be okay," He said with a quivering voice. I could hear him playing with the change in his pocket out of nervousness.

"Uh-huh," I said with a soft tone. Many tears ran down my face.

"Hurry up and get better," his wife says. "We gonna be here for you when you need us. Call me if you need something. You know these men ain't gonna do much for you. And come get your church kids. They really miss you. I love you, you hear?" she said.

"Uh-huh." I replied with a soft voice and more tears ran down my face.

I could feel Pastor M squeeze my arm, and out of my swollen eyes, I could see him wipe his eyes. He tapped on the rail of my bed and I could hear his ring hitting the bed rail. His fingers touched my right bicep. His wife was on my left. I wondered what the heck my face looked like because their expressions concerned me. I was wheeled back to my room. I was alone and I was glad. My only view out the window was a brick wall. I must have slept all day because when I opened my eyes, it was dark outside. I heard my door open. It was my husband. Someone was with him. I opened my eyes and saw it was our youth minister.

"Don't wake her up." I heard him say.

He stepped behind my husband. I remember hearing him pray over me, and then he was gone. I woke up during the night and saw his business card on my tray. The reconstruction was successful. For the next forty-eight hours, my pulse in the new breast was to be checked every fifteen minutes by a nurse. This meant I didn't get much sleep. I had many nurses but my favorite was Quincy. She was really sweet and kindhearted. I was not able to eat or drink much because I was still in a critical stage.

"Where is my husband?" I asked her.

"He went to the café for coffee," she said.

One of my nurses was from Nigeria. She was always singing when she entered the room. She checked my pulse and all of my vitals when Quincy was not there. While the nurse was in the bathroom, I decided to take a look at my body under the sheet. My tummy was flat, like it was when I was a teenager, and my new breast was shaped like the perfect orange on a tree. I nodded with approval and covered myself back up with the sheet. My husband entered the room with coffee in hand.

"How are the kids?" I asked.

"They're fine. They're with my mom," he said.

"I miss them," I said.

"I'm sure they miss you too," he replied.

For the next thirty-six hours, only nurses and doctors came in to check my pulse. It was strong and steady. I was tired and so was my body. My mind was wandering often. I thought of so many things I wanted to do when I got home. Now that I was slimmer, I wondered if I could fit those wishful-hopefuls in the back of my closet. I slept a lot off and on. Mainly between the checkups. I was past the forty-eight-hour mark and declared successful and I could eat something light like Jell-O and broth. Nonetheless, they continued to check my pulse every fifteen minutes. My husband had gone home at my request to check on the kids. They hadn't seen him for a couple days.

During the fifty-sixth hour, a devastating change happened. Quincy could no longer find the pulse in my breast. She checked in several spots but was not successful. She ran to get another nurse for her to check, then a doctor, then my surgeon. None of them could find the pulse. My doctor confirmed the reconstructive surgery failed and they had to take me back to the operating room immediately before an infection set in from the dead flesh that was inside the reconstructed breast. Quincy began to cry. The other nurses who were assisting were crying as well. I stopped for a moment and spoke to them.

"Everyone! Crying is not allowed in my presence," I said loudly.

"We're sorry," they said together and continued to unplug all the machines to take me to the OR

"Don't cry, Quincy," I said. "It's God's will."

"I'm so sorry, Laura. I'm so sorry," she said through a shaky voice.

"Hey! It wasn't up to you. You had no control over it. It's okay," I assured her.

"Laura, is there anyone we should call?" Quincy asked.

"Yes. Call my pastor and my husband," I responded.

"What's the number to the church?" she asked. There was no time to get my chart due to the nature of the situation. I gave her the numbers from memory and they began to prep me. My surgeon stood at my left side.

"I'm sorry, Laura, but we've gotta take you back," he said.

"I know," I said with tears in my eyes.

I remembered I couldn't cry because Quincy would cry and I didn't want my nose to get clogged. I needed it to be clear so they could place the breathing tubes in for oxygen. I did a self-talk while multiple nurses worked on me and around me to get me ready for surgery. They were ready to begin and so was I. I prayed for peace of mind for myself and God heard me. I was also glad they took that hot bag off of me. I was sweating.

"Goodbye, Quincy," I said to her. "Thank you for everything."

As I entered the operating room again, as always, I looked around. There were too many machines this time. I was thrown around like a rag doll, probably because this was life-threatening with the dead flesh inside of me.

"Laura. I need you to count backward from one hundred like last time," someone said.

They dragged me onto a new gurney quickly.

"One hundred, 99, 98, and so on," I said.

"Let's go, guys! She's out!" I heard someone say.

I woke up in much more pain than before. I was back in my room. I heard multiple machines around me. Some were above my head, to my right, to my left, and at the foot of my bed. I was afraid again. I didn't understand what was going on. I heard those footsteps again, and this time, they sounded heavier. It was my pastor. I could smell his cologne and hear him crying. He couldn't talk. He just squeezed my arm a few times and left.

After he left, my husband came in. My eyes were swollen because they were taped shut during surgery. My throat was very raw from the tube being down my throat. And I was thinking it would go down my nose. My legs felt trapped and my right arm was wrapped up. My finger had something on it as well tracking my pulse. I was later told by my surgeon that the surgery should have only taken four hours but I was under for nine hours. He was trying to save the breast by using one of my veins from my leg but my body rejected it repeatedly. He didn't want to lose that pulse again so he kept trying to save it. I also found out the reason why my pastor was so sad when he came by. He was told over the phone, "We lost her pulse and are taking her back to surgery immediately!" It wasn't that my heartbeat was gone. I lost the pulse in the breast that was reconstructed. Poor Quincy. Bless her heart. She was probably so shaken when she made those calls. When I was coherent, my surgeon came to see me.

"Laura. I tried to save the breast but I couldn't," he said.

"It's okay. At least it lasted for fifty-six hours," I said.

"We have you on heavy pain medication called morphine right now. Any time you need it, just push the button to your right and it will drip down. The glorified leg warmers are to keep your circulation going so you don't get a blood clot. If you were to develop a clot, it could go to your heart and kill you. This machine here is taking your blood pressure and this here is tracking your pulse and activity of your heart. This was my first failing TRAM flap and I don't know what else to say," he said.

"Nothing else you can say, doctor. God had a plan," I said.

Even though my response was not what he wanted to hear, he accepted it. It was not meant for me to have a breast on that side anymore.

"I know this isn't the time or place but you still have other options should you reconsider later down the road," he said.

I had much time to think about what had transpired over the last few days. Somehow I managed to have my cell phone and saw a text from Jonathan. It was his last game before Christmas break.

He wrote, "I'm dedicating tonight's game to you, Mom."

I cried. He didn't know about the new surgery and I didn't want to tell him because I did not want him to lose focus on his game from worrying about me. Jedidiah was not told because he would be angry and possibly blame God. My husband said he was not leaving again until I came home from the hospital. I did not disagree with him this time.

It was the night/early morning of December 15, 2006. The glorified leg warmers were making me hot and I wanted to take off some of the blankets. I was thinking about what I'd been through. Not only in the past few days but life in general. It seemed as if trouble found me regardless of what I did. *I must be pretty special*, I thought to myself. I chuckled a bit at the thought. I looked around my room.

My husband was asleep on the chair by the door and the nurses in the hall were moving in a synchronized fashion, almost as if they were programmed to do so. I tilted my head to the left just a little bit when everything changed.

And now, my ninth-hour experience.

I looked up at the clock and it was 2:00 a.m., on the dot. There was a deafening tone throughout my room. I couldn't hear my machines or the nurses outside in the hallway. My husband was still asleep on the chair and I was wondering why he hadn't awakened. I felt a presence like no other. The Holy Spirit was here. I immediately started talking to the Lord. I asked, "There's a testimony here, isn't it?"

Still talking to the Lord, I went on to apologize for things that I had done wrong prior to this day. I apologized for things I hadn't done and things that I won't mention in this story. But I knew He forgave me. And I know the prayer requests that I had before I entered into this fight were being taken care of. It was now exactly 2:15 a.m. and this was where my true healing began. I was already crying while I was apologizing to the Lord and I began to feel fingers on my left breast. Or should I say, where my left breast used to be. The hand began to examine my left-breast area. If you're a woman, you know how the ob-gyns do the examination. Well, it was the same type of exam, only this was being done by the Holy Spirit Himself. Then while the left side was being done, I felt fingers now on my right breast. It was as if they were both being examined for cancer. I was still crying and staring at the clock. While the one hand was still healing my right breast, I felt a hand go inside of my left breast area and lift the tissue up and then together. This happened over and over. It was as if my breast was being rebuilt in the shape that it was supposed to be in.

There were now two hands working on my left and one still working on my right. I took my eyes off of the clock to see if I could see the hands but I couldn't see anything but me. But I could feel the Holy Spirit's presence in my room along with the angels He brought with Him, and the hands were still at work on me. Now while the hands on my left-breast area was still working, the hand that was on my right breast had moved to my foot. Remember I told you the surgeon took a vein out of my foot. It was hurting me but it was wrapped up so that I wouldn't get a blood clot. So now while the hands were working on my left breast, the other hand was working on my left foot. I was getting the foot massage of a lifetime. My toes were swollen to the point of me not being able to spread them.

After the foot massage, still getting the work done on my left-breast area, the hands moved to my left hand. It was swollen from both surgeries. My fingers hurt because they were so big. I then got a hand massage by His hands. After the hand massage and the same hands were still working on my left-breast area, the other hand went back to my right breast and began to work on it some more as if to make sure everything was done right. I was still staring at the clock, guys. I was still crying and all I could say through my tears was, "Thank you, thank you, thank you."

I turned my head and saw, out of my peripheral, a vision. It was the silhouette of a man. It kind of startled me, but when I realized who He was, I was fine. Okay, back to staring at the clock. Just then, the hands had finished what they had come to do. I had gotten one last check on both sides and then it stopped. It was now 3:15 a.m. exactly! Still all I could say, with tears in my eyes, was, "Thank you, Jesus!"

After all of that, I told the Lord that I didn't want any more morphine because I had an allergic reaction to it and my body was itching all of the time. I asked him to please take my pain away because I didn't want to be drugged up and dependent on it. Immediately the pain was gone. I fell asleep and had the weirdest dream ever. And through that dream, I was shown the reason the cancer returned in the same breast. There was something more I needed to learn that I didn't the first time. He has my attention now. The Lord showed me that I would be giving my testimony in front of thousands of women one day. I don't know where or when but I am looking forward to it. And now again, all I can say is, "Thank you, Lord."

The next morning, I was excited about what I had experienced. I told my husband when he woke up. I'm not sure if he fully understood. I then told my nurse about it. She was just as puzzled. The nurse took my vital signs and checked my morphine drip.

"Why aren't you using the pain medications, Laura?" she asked.

"Remember, I told you I was healed in the night? I don't need it anymore. Matter of fact, I haven't felt any pain since 3:15 am. God healed me!" I said with excitement.

"I'll let the doctor know," she said in disbelief.

I didn't care that she didn't believe me. All I knew was I was touched by the hand of God through His angels. He stood at the foot of my bed while all of this was taking place. I couldn't look at Him, only see the silhouette from my peripherals.

"Is Quincy here today?" I asked the nurse.

"Quincy will be in tonight. I'll let her know you want to see her," she said.

"Thank you."

After the nurse finished checking my vital signs, she began talking to my husband. I don't know what they discussed. I was still basking in the glow of healing. I had a ninth-hour experience and I wanted to share it with whoever would listen to me. Later that day, a different oncologist came to see me. She stated that the margins were clear after the TRAM flap failed. After removing the dead tissue, they had to do a full scrape to ensure all the dead flesh was gone and no surrounding tissues were affected.

"Do you want to go home, Laura?" she asked.

"Yes, ma'am. I do."

"Well, you're gonna have to get up and walk so that your muscles can get some exercise and blood flow," she said. "The nurses will bring you a walker to assist you."

The nurses brought me a walker with tennis balls at the bottom of each leg. I felt like a senior citizen. While I was walking, my husband told me that there was a prayer vigil going on in the waiting room when I went back into surgery. My church family, immediate family, and friends were sitting and standing wall-to-wall. There was no place left for anyone to stand who came in. Nurses also told me they felt the power of God in that place and that I have a lot of people who care about me. I couldn't help but smile.

The effects of the morphine caused me to feel itchy and I had nurses scratching my back most of the day and night. Quincy was back, and often, she would put lotion on my back because she thought it was dry. Turns out, I had an allergic reaction to the morphine.

"How are you feeling, Laura?" she asked.

"Fine," I told her. "Quincy. Thank you for taking care of me. I know it's your job but you've been doing things for me that I've done for myself since I was a little girl. I'm not ashamed but just feel helpless a bit. Thanks for your professionalism."

"I don't think I was very professional a few days ago when we had to take you back to surgery. That was my first experience with a TRAM flap failure."

"It didn't fail. It just wasn't meant to be. But God healed me completely during the wee hours. It was wonderful," I said.

Quincy was not a Christian but she respected all religions and allowed me to tell her my story.

"Wow! That's amazing!" she said.

"Yup! It is!"

Through all of the excitement and me being able to walk for the first time with the walker, I'd forgotten to look under my gown. When the second surgery first happened, I didn't want to look for fear of what I might *not* see. Now I was ready. I was alone in the room and looked under my gown. I had six plastic bulbs dangling from plastic tubes placed in my body. Four ran hip to hip and the other two were coming from the breast that had the mastectomy. I began to feel sick looking at what happened. My breast was really gone. While I pondered that, I was reminded of what God had done to me and for me in the night. I just lay there, quietly reflecting. I was now able to eat real food but nothing too solid.

Two of the church members snuck in to see me. It was good to have company. My hair was falling out due to the stress my body had undergone in the past week. I was still itching but it wasn't as bad. I was able to get to the restroom without help but I still had the glorified leg warmers on. Each time I stood up, I lifted my gown up to see my body shape. When I went in on December 12, I weighed 170 pounds. By the time I left the hospital, I weighed 150 pounds. The doctor said with the TRAM flap, losing a breast, and not being able to eat, the weight was gone. But I still had a ways to go for a full recovery. I didn't care. I was healed and this was all just a process.

I was finally allowed to go home. I was ready. I'd taken pictures with my nurses and my doctors. This was Quincy's day off but I left her a card with the nurses, saying thank you for everything and that I would never forget her. When Quincy was on shift and she'd check in on me every fifteen minutes, we would talk about her home country, the Philippines, and how hard she'd worked to become a nurse. She spoke a little of Tagalog to me and I wanted to learn more. We talked about my kids, my church, and music. The Nigerian nurse came in singing and gave me a hug. She told everyone all of the messy things she did for me. She was a sweetheart and this was one place I would not miss anytime soon.

The fresh air and sunshine felt good on my face. When I got home, my sister Liz was there. She greeted me at the door and gave me a kiss. I don't remember where the kids were at the time but I was anxious to see them. I sat downstairs for a while to rest my legs. The surgeon told me not to go up and down the stairs because my stitches could tear—no housework, cooking, or to lift anything larger than a dinner plate for four to eight weeks. Our apartment looked different. Or maybe I was looking at things differently since I was touched by the Lord's hands. One encounter with Him made all the difference in my world.

My babies were home now. I was glad to see them and they me. They had a lot of questions. Questions I couldn't answer. We talked for a couple hours. They told me about school, their friends, and who got in trouble while I was away. It was all music to my ears. After some time had passed, it was time for me to go to bed. Since I still had a ways to go for a full healing, I had to choose where I would sit or lie. Once I was upstairs, I was not coming back down and the same for going downstairs. The kids took turns walking behind me as I took the stairs. Part of it was in case I fell backward or needed help, and the other part was when they did the TRAM flap surgery, they removed belly fat to create a new breast. While doing so, they cut through a lot of my nerves. I was left numb all the way round from my belly button in a full circle. The doctors said I may never get the full feeling back.

Because I lost so much weight, my pants would fall down and I couldn't feel it. We came up with the code word *Uh-oh* so that I would know to look down and pull up my pants. It was quite funny until it happened in public. To this day, I still can't feel much in that area.

I STUFF MY BRA... SO WHAT?

"Why are you walking so slow, Mommy?" Mara asked.

"Because I have an owie," I answered.

She had a puzzled look on her face but didn't ask for more information, and I was glad she didn't. I had to have a step stool at my bedside to get in and out of the bed. I had six pillows surrounding me for comfort. The bulbs had to be drained and the contents recorded daily.

Initially I hated doing this. I began to get angry because if the surgery hadn't failed, I wouldn't be doing this right now. In the first forty-eight hours, after draining the bulbs, I raised my shirt to see my scars. Now I looked like one of the women from the videos—a cut-and-paste model. I let out a heavy sigh. Constantly I was reminded of the healing I had received. I believe it was God's way of speaking to my heart, to have a heart of gratefulness. Many have tackled this and faced worse and some did not have the opportunity because they died.

My first few nights were challenging. I didn't sleep much. I couldn't get comfortable. I was beginning to hurt in the areas where the bulbs were. This was because they were filled with fluid and would sometimes dangle which pulled on the flesh of my breast area. Getting up at night to use the restroom was rough without the bars on the bed as I'd had in the hospital. Some nights, I would cry silently out of frustration. I needed and wanted help but I didn't want to wake anyone up. I had three meals a day, thanks to Liz serving me and some of the church members bringing food to the house. I received many cards and flowers. My friends who sew made me a blue blanket and booties to match. It made me so happy.

It was time for a field trip. I went to the store with Liz. The sun on my face felt wonderful. I missed it. I walked too slow for her so I had to ride in a motorized wheelchair. I also needed to wear a mask in public because of germs. I got a taste of what it's like for those who must use that type of transportation on a regular basis. Some people were very rude and wouldn't allow me to pass. Others saw the mask and the wheelchair and let me go ahead of them. I used my dad's handicap placard for the trip so I wouldn't have to walk too far to the entrance. I received many stares from people outside whose facial expressions questioned if I had a reason to use the placard.

If they ask me I'll just raise my shirt and show them my scars and bulbs, I thought to myself.

Liz stayed with me for three weeks. I hated when the time came for her to leave. My husband took her to the airport. I cried like Nettie in the movie *The Color Purple* when she and her sister were separated because of Mister.

"Call me if you need me," she said.

I closed the front door and quickly grabbed my phone and dialed her cell number.

"Yes?" Liz answered.

"I need you! Come back!" I said through my quivering voice and tears.

"I love you. I'll call you when I get to my gate," she said.

After we hung up the phone, I got it in my mind to work harder on strengthening my body. I slowly made my way up the stairs. The kids were not there to assist me so I went up backward while sitting like toddlers do. I knelt down by my side of the bed and prayed. When I was finished, I had a new perspective. A few new goals and I was reminded of what God showed me in the dream when I was in the hospital. I knew why the cancer returned. During times of loss, I chose some unhealthy and healthy practices. The second bout was a reminder to rid myself of those practices once and for all. Now I had to act.

"I see you, God. I've learned. Help me stay focused," I said out loud. The future was filled with potential and promise. I was determined not to let Him down again.

Chapter 12

BRA-STUFFING 101

My new normal was draining bulbs, cleaning tubes, and learning to walk upright. Standing up straight hurt my abdominal muscles. And it allowed the bulbs in my breast and abdominal area to dangle without hurting. I wasn't confident enough yet. I called the doctor and was told to walk with my shoulders back as best I could. The muscles needed to heal and all the layers they cut through needed to as well. The woman who worked with me after my lumpectomy in 2001 came to the house to show me the new type of bras for mastectomy patients. It looked like a fancy undershirt with pockets. The material was very soft. It felt like it had two-thousand-count cotton in it. She showed me how to get dressed and where to store the bulbs so that I could sleep comfortably and walk around without feeling like one would fall out. I was very appreciative of her. I found out that she'd also helped my mother with her bras. That made me smile. I could not be fitted for a prosthesis/breast form until the bulbs were removed and that wasn't for three more weeks or until the drainage stopped.

The bulbs were finally removed and I got my breast form. It was like folding a silicone taco and trying to place it in a sock. *Very odd*, I thought. I lost about seven more pounds once I got home from the hospital. This was due to the shock to my system as well as not being able to eat more solid foods. I was afraid to eat things like chicken, steak, or heavy potatoes. To be honest, I didn't want to gain the weight back. But mostly, my system didn't seem to care for those types of foods at the time. It's an amazing thing to be in a body that has gone through such trauma, witness the healing process spiritually, and physically have to watch and experience the inward healing all at the same time. I found myself looking for the tattoos they'd placed on me five years prior. They were still there but not as visible. To this day, I can only find six of them. I believe the seventh is tucked away with the other skin where my breast used to be.

The year 2007 went by quickly. My oldest son graduated from high school and prepared for college. My other children were growing so fast and they were so smart. My marriage wasn't as strong as it once was but we were trying. The kids' schedules were hectic, and some days, I was too tired to be with them. Thank God for my in-laws because on particular days, I couldn't be outside. My white blood count was low and I was advised against being in the sun for too long, to rest often, pay attention to what I ate, and to drink plenty of water. I still had trouble sleeping but it wasn't because I was uncomfortable. It was because I was worried about being a whole woman. Part of the former conversation about the mastectomy with my spouse was going through my mind. I was feeling insecure and I spoke with Pastor M on the phone about it.

"That isn't what makes you a woman," he said.

"I know but—"

"But nothing. Your body went through a traumatic experience. In short, we did too when we thought we would lose you. Take your time. Let God do what only He can do. If you have any trouble, let me know," he said.

"Thanks, pastor."

He and I never spoke on the phone for very long. This was a busy season so he was short and to the point. I thought back to my early days of stuffing my bra, I laughed. There I was, a child, trying to be something I wasn't to impress people who didn't care, to be someone I wasn't. Then I get older and have to stuff my bra anyway. And I still have trouble doing it because if the taco doesn't go in right,

I'll look lopsided. I felt like a trick artist. All the moving and shifting I had to do to get that thing in the pocket. Folding and shaping it, making sure I was even on both sides was ridiculous. It took me back to my bulky paper-breast days. If I could, I wouldn't wear it at all. I also used to use the phrase "You look like a cancer patient" to my brothers after a bad haircut very often. God has a sense of humor.

As the months passed, I got used to wearing the breast form. At least, I thought I did. I received many questions about my experience. I called some of the people back who'd helped me along the way and shared my story. They were shocked but not surprised at what God can do. My dad and I began to have Sunday dinner at his favorite restaurants twice a month. My upper-body strength came back slower than my lower-body strength. Carrying anything heavier than twenty-five pounds was hard but I was determined to get stronger.

Later in the year, I called Mrs. Jones, Ricky's mom, to see how she was doing and him as well. She told me Ricky passed away from complications of pneumonia. He was sick for a very long time. I was very sad to hear this. We'd lost touch for quite some time after our last phone call. Mrs. Jones had remarried and was doing well. I told her about my children and my health scares and promised to keep in touch as often as I could.

I got a job at a local grocery store. I wanted to have some pocket money of my own. About six weeks into the job, I was out retrieving shopping carts. I said a silent prayer to God that if He got me outta this job, I would go back to school. As soon as I said amen, I was walking in the parking lot and I was almost hit by a white Cadillac. After the driver parked, an older African-American man got out. He was old-school, a smooth walker, and a smooth talker.

"Hey, little lady. How are you?" he asked. I guess he didn't realize he almost ran me over.

"I'm fine. How are you?" I said with a big smile on my face.

"Good. Say, where's your manager?"

"The store manager is gone for the day but I can give him a message if you like."

"I want to tell them what a wonderful job you're doing out here, gettin' these baskets."

"Aww, thank you, sir!" I said, still with a big smile on my face.

"Naw, I'm playin'," he said. "Go back to school!" Then he walked into the store as if we'd never spoke. I was surprised at what he said. My mouth was hanging open. I pushed the baskets to the coral, turned around, and waited for him to come out of the store. He never came out and his Cadillac was gone. I was convinced that I was visited by an angel. I immediately ran into the store and told my Christian coworker what happened.

"You know what that means, right?" she said.

"Yup! It's time to give my two-week notice to leave," I told her.

"I'll be right behind you. I wanna go back to school too."

I turned in my notice the next day. I was browsing on the Internet and a university site popped up. I clicked it, gave my name and number, and received a call within an hour. I met with an enrollment counselor the next week and enrolled for the upcoming semester. The entire program would be online which was perfect because I wanted to be home for my family. Each course was nine weeks. I was determined to finish and not take any breaks.

The program was stringent. There were many times I wanted to quit but God gave me the strength to keep going. I wanted my children to be proud of me. I wanted my parents to be proud of me, but mostly, I wanted to make God proud. He'd saved my life and gave me a complete healing. I couldn't stop now. I graduated in May 2010, with a bachelor's degree in human services management.

Since the second surgery and my ninth-hour experience, my faith in God grew stronger and my relationship deeper. Deeper than I knew until God spoke to me again. This time, it had to do with a reveal. For a few years after the surgery, I was very insecure about my husband seeing me fully naked. I remembered what he'd said prior to my mastectomy, what my pastor said about that being something that does not define me as a woman, and what God said. In a sense, I was starting over. It was hard for me to trust because of my past. God was rebuilding me and I couldn't see how He was going to do it.

In the dream, God showed me I needed to get undressed completely in front of my husband as an intimate way to show him I trusted him. Initially I didn't trust Him and wouldn't do it but the spiritual nagging wouldn't go away. I finally did it. I revealed myself to him completely and God showed me that he was not ready nor prepared to handle the new me, my struggle, and my spiritual growth. This placed an even tougher strain on my marriage. But I continued to trust God. Daily I went to my church at 5:00 a.m. and prayed. Some days, I lay on my face. Other days, I would walk around the sanctuary, singing and praising Him.

On rainy days, I would sit in front of the pulpit on the floor and just look up with my eyes closed to hear Him speak to me. Things I learned during these times, I taught my children and my godchildren—perseverance through tough times and, mostly, how to fully trust God even though we can't trace Him. I had men and women in my life who kept me accountable by checking in with me regularly via phone calls, e-mails, and text messages. They prayed for me and with me. I was given godly advice about staying strong, multiple scriptures to read for encouragement, and some visited when they could.

A year later, I had many opportunities to speak at breast-cancer awareness events at colleges, women events and churches. Though the crowds weren't large, the message reached them and I was happy to share my story if it meant someone's life will be changed for the better. After speaking at one of the colleges, a man came to me and said thank you for sharing. He and his wife were struggling after her diagnosis and surgery. He was accused often of not being sensitive enough to her and what she was going through. After hearing me speak, he had a better understanding and said he can become a better husband, friend, and support for her. That was news to my ears. I wasn't as informed as I probably should have been, considering what I'd gone through, but I remember my youth minister telling me that the one thing no one can take away from you is your testimony. My experience and what God did in it was all I had to share, and I prayed He would use it to His glory.

There was still so much to learn about stuffing my bra properly. I just figured if you got the right materials and put them in correctly, all would fall into place. Not true. For instance, when I would go to the gym, I couldn't wear a traditional sports bra. I had new gear so I had to do some things differently like wear a regular bra with a sports bra to keep the separation obvious.

I didn't like the fact that the prosthesis would shift when jumping, and sometimes, I ended up wearing two bras for one breast. That made no sense to me but it was necessary. A reality check for myself came when I worked out intensely. The sweat running down my body was like someone had poured a giant cup of water over me. But when I went into the locker room, only one side of my shirt was wet. I remember in my 5:00-a.m. cycling class, there was a woman named Jeannie. Jeannie was clearly a survivor. What I mean by clearly is she didn't wear a sports bra or prosthesis. She simply wore her fitted workout shirt as she was, lopsided and all. And she wore it proudly! That was very inspiring to me. She used to call me little girl as a joke because she thought I was still wet behind the ears and didn't know much about life. I never shared with her about my cancer but listened to her each time she spoke—as if every word was important regardless of what she spoke of. She was a warrior! She was not afraid of her scars! I wanted to be like her.

I joined a local support group who got me thinking beyond my diagnosis. I created a vision board and wrote some things down as focal points, goals for me to reach while I continue this journey. I placed pictures of foreign countries I wanted to visit, activities I wanted to take part in like skydiving, rock climbing, and especially waterskiing, and, of course, more marathons. God had given me more than a second chance. I also wanted to write a book about my journey and, if needed, walk through this fight with other men and women should they need me.

During my new five-year remission, I participated in therapy to work on myself. I had so much going on at home with my children and juggling it on the outside was easy. Mentally it was exhausting. I sought guidance through Pastor G. He explained that my journey is just that, my journey. And I was not to try and walk someone else's because it wasn't designed for me. What he said made sense but applying that daily was difficult. If you remember, I repeatedly compared myself to my older sister Dee-Dee in ways that shouldn't have mattered. Being the youngest of nine children and a girl was a challenge. I was always the last to know the important changes about the family and it made me feel insignificant.

I know that the Word says I am fearfully and wonderfully made, but the enemy is real; and when he knows your weaknesses, he will use them against you to bring you lower than you already are. Once in a while, it worked. Through therapy, fasting and praying, and journaling I gained confidence. I looked at myself in a new way. I was more assertive at work. My creative juices were flowing and I was writing again. I finished a book several years prior and left it on the shelf. I had more new ideas now, new titles floating around, new songs, new pictures in my head. I was excited and giddy about what God was developing within me. Many times, I would pray and ask God what to do next. I didn't get direct answers but I figured, as long as I kept talking to Him while watching and waiting, He would eventually answer. I had the faith He would.

During this part of the journey, my two older sons had already joined the military—the air force and the army. My twins, Deion and Derick, were in their junior year in high school, and Mara was in her last year of junior high. Once in a while, they would ask questions about when I was sick. I felt I was doing them a favor by not bringing them into the conversation about my health back then. I later learned that was not a good idea. Children feel their parents' stress and see more than we know. I told them I was diagnosed with breast cancer but that God healed me completely and I would be fine.

After that second surgery, the kids did not come into the room often to see me. I didn't want them to see my tubes and bulbs dangling. I didn't have answers for them. Once in a while, they'd stand at the door to say good night to me but did not get to hug me as they'd done before. Hugging was painful then, but how was I supposed to tell them their hugs hurt? I thought it was ironic that I fell into the same pattern when I went through my second bout with cancer—repeating the same behavior by not allowing the kids to see what I went through and by not telling them the truth all along. The three little pigs, lovingly nicknamed, said that they should have been told and that they were old enough to understand. I apologized for not telling them and they forgave me.

Since I was that little girl, I have learned that stuffing bras is an art. One has to have serious skills to do it properly. It takes accurate planning, placement, steady materials, the right gear, codes and such, and a sharp eye for symmetry. People know when something isn't done correctly, when something is off. Just as my children knew I was hiding something by the way I was acting, moving slowly, and talking in code. Going through my second battle with breast cancer allowed my children to witness how God changed me inside and out. That was the push they needed to be successful at whatever was placed in their path.

There was a time when the doctors wanted to run tests on Mara to see if she had the BRCA gene, the breast cancer gene. My mother was still alive when this first came up and disagreed. When the cancer was found again, I was asked again about the testing but I declined. I told them I would keep my daughter informed of our health history and my battles, and if she wanted to go through with it as an adult, that would be her choice. I also told them from what I know about *my* God, He hears and answers prayers. My prayers were that the cancer stopped and stayed with me and not affect the next generations. I believe it's already done!

UNDERWIRE BRAS

*This bra creates breast separation and
brings them closer to the chest.*

After getting back to my routine, the tone of my household changed. My husband and I separated in late 2012. I was blessed to find an apartment in the same school district so the three little pigs wouldn't have to change schools. I did my best to keep some normalcy in their lives. Throughout this transition, staying connected with God's Word brought me closer to Him in a way I hadn't before. Even when I was shown to reveal myself back in 2009 and that created an openness with Him, this was a deeper and tighter relationship. Daily I read my Bible, walked and prayed each morning while working three jobs. God arranged for all of my pay periods to fall on the same day so that we would lack nothing. I also tithed with each paycheck. I watched my children mature. They were no longer bickering daily. Their time was shared between their dad and me and they began watching out for one another more and hanging out together nearly every day. Because I worked three jobs, my workdays lasted into the evenings, sometimes until 9:00 p.m. Since the three had grown closer together and to God, I knew I didn't have to worry about them. This allowed me to rest better and stay focused at work.

The following week, I'd gone to my next oncology checkup and was advised to keep my habits in check. Meaning I had to do my best not to engage in activities that would cause me a lot of stress. I needed my numbers to stay medium to high. See, when undergoing treatment for cancer, my red and white blood cell count must stay within a certain range. The red blood cells carry oxygen through the body. The white cells fight infection. Whenever I would have a low white count, this usually meant I wasn't resting enough or stressed out. Should they get too low, my doctor would place me on medications to keep them at a normal range. Much of the stress was due to work, my marital status, and my children. I was also taking care of my daddy during this time. In essence, I had four jobs.

One of the worst side effects I was now facing was when my mastectomy area would ache. If I could describe it, I'd say it was like having arthritis in my chest wall. It was explained to me as such: when someone undergoes the surgery I had, it takes time for the muscles to regroup and heal so when I'd get cold, that area would hurt bad enough where I had to lie down. If I was in a place where lying down was not possible, I would try and cover my chest up with a sweater or jacket if I had one. Also I would have to lean in the opposite direction of where the pain was to release the pressure from my left side. Sounds weird, I know, but it's what helped me each time. There were days when the pain was relentless and I had to cancel particular outings with family and friends. I called my oncologist about it and he scheduled an ultrasound for me. He wanted to be sure there wasn't a tumor there or that they missed something during surgery. Again I was a little anxious, even though I knew I'd been healed.

I went into a room the size of a standard household bathroom but it had two doors to enter and exit. I was assigned to a young woman who had apparently never done an ultrasound. I was already in my gown when she came in and lying on my back with my gown closed. When she opened the gown, her face froze. She paused and gasped at the same time. Poor thing, she was nearly in tears. I would have to guess that they didn't tell her about my health status.

Nonetheless, I assured her to move forward and I was okay. She wiped her eyes, put on her purple gloves, grabbed the sonogram gel to place it on me. The gel ran down my side. I could tell she was nervous. I wiped it off, told her to try again, and pretend she was putting lotion on me and to squirt it directly on to the empty spot. She then pushed the green button to signal for the doctors to come in. The young lady gladly stepped aside to allow the doctors to check me.

The good news was they only saw scar tissue and muscle. The bad news was this pain would continue for quite some years. My doctors said that area is like a honeycomb with multiple combs healing all at the same time. It's sensitive to heat and cold. If the pain got too bad, I was instructed to take an aspirin. The hip-to-hip surgery site was still numb all the way around. But somehow, I managed to feel the inside of my stomach and belly button now. My belly button was repositioned during the second surgery, and when he closed the area, he made it into the shape of a heart. I thought that was very fitting. I could feel itching on the inside which frustrated me often, but since I could not scratch the outside, I had to pat the area. One of my new tricks was to psych myself out and make my mind think it was scratching the actual area so I could have some relief. This technique also worked when I would rub my stomach after I ate too much. Because I had no feeling on the outside, I had to look down to confirm I was touching that particular area. There were times when I would feel a buzzing in my stomach area, and if I had my cell phone on me and it was on vibrate, I would miss a lot of calls. The buzzing feeling came from my nerves trying to reconnect and, oftentimes, I couldn't tell the difference between the two.

For every ache and pain, I would get a little afraid of what it meant. I often read my life passage, Isaiah 41:10, to stay focused. It says, "Fear not for I am with thee. Be not dismayed for I am thy God. I will strengthen thee; yea I will help thee; yea, I will uphold thee with the right hand of my righteousness." Other women who I'd shared my experience with would pray with me and for me. I still went to therapy with Pastor G and he would give me scriptures and devotionals to read as well as recommended another support group at his church that I might be interested in. I didn't attend the group because I got tired of sharing my story. That's when God did a body check on me to remind me of His deliverance.

It was a weeknight and I was very tired. I had been away from the house for fifteen hours and was ready to go to bed. I said my prayers, and as I got settled into my bed, I could not sleep. I tossed and turned. I tried praying some more, hoping that would help, but nothing. I sat up in my bed and said, "Lord, why can't I sleep?" It was like a movie ran across my wall, showing me what I'd been healed from. This is the LAMF translation of what God said, "You don't wanna share, huh? Too tired, huh? Okay." I immediately rolled over on my knees and prayed again.

This time, I asked for forgiveness and told the Lord, "I'll do whatever you want and share whenever you want." One would have thought I was about to get a butt whoopin'. My heavenly Father gave me a reminder to get me out of my comfort zone. The next day, I was exhausted when I went to work. A woman came into my office, inquiring about a class we had to offer. After I gave her the information and had her fill out the paperwork to enroll, she began talking about her breast cancer diagnosis. She was thirty-five years old, newly married, had a seven-year-old, and had a small baby on her hip. She started telling me she had so many unanswered questions. She started to cry.

"Can I pray with you?" I asked.

"Please do," she said.

As we went into prayer, I could feel the Holy Spirit surround us. She began crying more, possibly sensing it as well. After the prayer, she hugged me.

"Thank you for the prayers," she said.

"You're welcome."

I went on to tell her a little about my journey with breast cancer and gave her some questions to ask her oncologist. I told her of the different options that may be available regarding surgery and how she needed to write down all of her concerns prior to each appointment and to take someone with her, if possible. Sometimes we get sidetracked and forget until we've already left the doctor's office.

"Thanks again for your advice and prayers. God bless you," she said.

"You're welcome. Take care," I responded.

After the woman left, I looked up and smiled. "I hear you, Lord," I said.

God was not only using me to minister to other women on this continuous journey but to bring me closer to Him. I don't know how I thought just because I was healed, I was done doing anything for God. During this time, many of the friends and family I was close to were no longer reaching out to me. It was me who did the calling, texting, e-mailing, writing, and visiting to check on them. When I initially got the second diagnosis, folks were beating down my door to see me, talk to me, text, and call.

It may be because they thought I was going to die. Once I got better, things changed. I believe God uses it all in a way for us to get closer to Him. I don't hold anything against those who walked away. People get busy and forget. Some people can't handle that type of diagnosis such as I had.

Almost twice per month, my path would cross with a male or female dealing with some type of cancer. I couldn't escape it and I no longer wanted to. I would share things on my social media page as encouragement. I still had three paying jobs, and at one location, I had a male resident come in to tell me of his wife's diagnosis. Since I was in another type of industry, I was careful about what I said and shared concerning cancer. Then I could hear that deafening sound again. The same one I'd heard while I was in the hospital. It's almost like someone said, "Cue the music," and I knew it was time for me to share my testimony with him. I don't know how long we talked but it was long enough for me to share a good summary. He too was having a hard time with the diagnosis, her choice to have a double mastectomy, and who would take care of the kids. His overall theme was, "What about me?" After he was done whining about his feelings, I simply asked a few questions.

"What would you do if she died?"

"I don't know," he said.

"I totally understand where you're coming from, but if she died, who would take care of the kids then?"

"I guess I would," he said. "My mother, her mother, and me."

"A big part of her died when she was diagnosed. A new part of her died when she was given the options available to her. She doesn't need to lose much more because you're scared. I would advise you to pray first then go back to her and apologize but tell her why you feel the way you do so she understands." I grabbed his hand and said, "Your kids and your wife are depending on you."

"I don't know if I can say all that but I'll try," he said.

"Well, I'll pray God gives you the strength to at least apologize then let the conversation go from there."

You may be thinking I was hard on him. I believe I was trying to stress to him how important it is for them to go through this together rather than apart. There are too many lives at stake when a diagnosis and suggested surgery like this are in play. I may have been a little too passionate about his participation. Nonetheless, after he let go of my hands, he said thank you and left. I had to pray he wouldn't report me to the company. I never heard anything about it so I guess all was well. I had become a rebel for the cause now. I did not want God to have to remind me again.

Here's something else that changed with my second diagnosis. I no longer wore V-neck shirts, low-cut blouses, see-through tops, or even tank tops. I was afraid someone would see my scars and tease me. I had a very hard time being comfortable wearing anything that may cause anyone to stare at my top area. What hasn't changed is when I tell anyone—male or female—I had breast cancer twice, they still look me up and down in my chest area. Truth be told, I am more comfortable naked than I am with clothes on. I once went to a spa where wearing clothing in the common area for women was optional. I gladly opted to wear nothing. It was like my coming-out party and I was no longer ashamed of my scars and lack of fullness. There was no longer anything to hide behind. My truth was just that. God brought me closer to His bosom. I have accepted it! I embraced it! I owned it!

LONGLINE: PUSH-UP BRAS

This type of bra can serve as a corset and a brassiere. The push-up bra lifts and supports the breasts and could create sexy cleavage.

I remember the first time I wore a Longline bra. I was a bridesmaid in my cousin's wedding and the dresses were strapless and an A-line style. I had laryngitis and couldn't talk. I didn't weigh much then either and thought I didn't need one, but my aunt would not have it. We all had to look uniform regardless. It reminded me of when I was little and trying to fit in with so many girls and young women. I was correctly proportioned and felt I didn't need to wear one. So I didn't put it on. That was until a male outside the family made a comment about the top portion of my dress and how mine looked smaller than the others. It hurt my feelings but I ran to the bathroom and put it on. This Longline bra not only smoothed me out but it had a push-up bra effect, creating a visual attractiveness. I liked what I saw. Since I had no voice, I couldn't talk back. What I did have was confidence and a great smile during the entire ceremony and reception. I was happy for my cousin.

Over the past few years, I have had to repeatedly check my feelings at the door with both men and women. Maybe it's the innocence in me but I generally think people are good but just aren't good at thinking before they speak or shielding their facial expressions. I hear plenty of insensitive things in different places regarding women and their breasts. I was at a local grocery store and overheard a couple arguing over the woman showing too much cleavage.

"You should cover up more," he said.

"Why?" she asked. "That's how I got you. You didn't mind then."

"That was different," he replied.

"How?" she asked. "It's true. Men are visual, and if I hadn't been wearing the low-cut blouse when I met you, you wouldn't have looked at me."

"That's only partially true," he said. "I remember seeing your face first but your breasts were a distraction."

"Well, maybe I should just get cancer then and have them cut off!" she stated.

"That's stupid!" he said. "I need you to have them."

I made it my business to get out of theirs. They were getting on my nerves. I hurried past them down a different aisle. I have to remember I am in a different place than other people *because* of what I have been through. I have made it a point to ignore it as best I can, to sit up straight as often as I can, and watch more than I speak. James 1:19 says, "My dear brothers and sisters, take note of this: Everyone should be quick to listen, slow to speak and slow to become angry" (KJV). I didn't always follow this but I tried.

I began taking care of my dad full-time in 2014. He was ninety-six years old and his diabetes was getting worse and he was growing weaker. When we sat together, he would challenge me on the Sunday sermon by asking me what it was about. I'd give him the sermon topic, scripture reference, and give him the points given. He would always ask me to expound on it. Many days, I could not give what he asked because he was looking for something in particular.

He was a simple man who loved God's Word. He wanted to be sure I was paying attention and not just writing the points down. While he was in his right mind, we'd discuss my health updates. He knew my numbers were good and my weight was up and that wasn't good. He encouraged me to take care of myself because when I get his age, it only gets harder. I bought my first car this same year. I drove it to his house so he could see it. Though he was a bit feeble, he walked outside, told me to open the door so he could see inside, and gave me the thumbs up. I remember sitting with him and him being restless. He was calling out Uncle Willie's name, his brother, often as well as his sister who'd passed on before him. Our last conversation went like this:

"I'm the last of my kind," he said. "I've outlived all of my generation. I've gone as far as I can go. God has allowed me to see more than I could ever have imagined. I have no regrets."

A couple months later, he passed away from kidney and heart failure. He died in his home with me at his side.

Planning Daddy's funeral was easy as far as paperwork was concerned. He paid for everything ahead of time and told me what he wanted done. Each time we talked, I would take notes on my phone to record his journey. At first, he frowned; but when I told him what I was doing, he agreed. He stood tall on purpose, even as an old man. Though he didn't wear a bra, I'm sure there were days when he needed some smoothing out and a push upward.

After all I know, I still found myself doubting some things. I'd come nearly eight years as a two-time breast-cancer survivor now. My health was good. My children were doing very well in most areas. The divorce was final now but I was doubting if I'd ever love again; if a man found me, would he love me for me? I thought back to Ricky Jones again. What must've been going on in his head to say the things he did to me and to follow me wherever I went? I'll never know because I never asked. God allowed love to find me a couple years later. I told him about my health scares, my past, and my insecurities.

"I don't care about any of that stuff. That doesn't make you a woman," he said. "Follow God's leading, consecrate yourself and see what He does. That's all."

It was nice to know there's a Ricky Jones still out there. Would he follow me wherever I go? We'll see.

A couple years later, I began to feel something moving in my stomach, a rumbling of sorts. It was like I had a baby moving inside, only I wasn't pregnant. I also felt a tugging near my belly button. It was very painful. I made an appointment to see the surgeon who'd done the TRAM flap in 2006. Just driving out to that hospital caused me to have anxiety. Remember I told you that any little ache and pain I had sent me to the doctor's office. When he came in, we hugged for a long time. I hadn't seen him since that year. We discussed the events that transpired back then.

"I still can't believe it. After I did your surgery, the next few years, all was fine. I only had two more fail since then," he said.

"Well, since I was the first, that makes me more special," I said.

"How can I help you?" he asked.

"I feel movement in my stomach and there's a pull coming from my navel area that really hurts. Can you check it out?"

He made my lie down on the table and I raised my blouse. He felt around and saw a lump sticking up.

"The movement you're feeling is your stomach muscles coming back together. They are attempting to regenerate. Remember, we cut through many layers when we did the TRAM flap and it takes years to heal. Now the pull you're feeling is also because of the nerves and muscles in that area. Remember I told you not to use anything in your navel area for cleaning, to let water go in and go out only? This is because this area will always be sensitive to touch. Even though it's been thirteen years, you're not done yet. Just give it more time. I don't see any cause for alarm. Your numbers are good but you do need to lose some weight."

I frowned when he said that because I knew it was true.

"Are you still working out?" he asked. "You're a runner, right?"

"Yeah. I'm running to the fridge," I said. "Can't you do another surgery to get rid of the belly fat again?" I asked.

"No. You're not a candidate. You need to be at least in the obese category to qualify. Just hit the gym and watch what you eat," he said. "Since you were here last, there are other options for reconstruction if you're ever interested again. So let me know."

"Thanks, doc! I'll think about it," I replied.

After walking out of the office, I felt confident again. My emotions were up and down the days leading up to seeing him again. I thought back to the pre-op and post-op days of 2006 and where everything changed. God had done a miracle in that place—in me—and I was treating it like something everyone goes through. I wondered how Quincy was doing and if she still works there. I wondered if I would ever choose to replace the breast I lost someday. I wondered a lot of things this day. On the way home, I prayed and asked God to show me a new thing. He did. He showed me part of the first vision concerning women again but with an addition. I knew exactly what he meant.

For weeks, I had visitors and vendors entering my office who had a cancer story. Some had just begun their journey, some were going through treatment, and some were in remission. It was amazing to see how God brought them my way. They were encouraging and others were not as hopeful because their family or friend had passed away. I did my best to offer encouraging words, some scripture if it was called for; but mostly, I gave the ministry of presence and listening. Sometimes people just want you to listen to their story, not necessarily give a solution. I was looking slim and supported now in a whole new way. I was also closer to God than I had been in a while.

I will always be a cancer survivor. All of this journey, especially my ninth-hour experience, showed me that the areas God healed will never suffer from that disease again. But that doesn't give me the right to neglect those areas. On December 15, 2019, I hit my thirteen-year anniversary of being cancer-free from my second diagnosis in 2006. To God be the glory!

FINAL THOUGHTS

As I come to a close, I am reminded of my start in life and what a challenge it was becoming Laura. I'll admit that parts of this journey could have been a little easier had I listened to grown folks who had more insight and wisdom than me and listened to possibly the only boy who loved me for me when I was ten years old, Ricky Jones. Many were placed along my path for guidance and leading, giving me multiple clues and warnings, but being impatient with others as well as with God and myself only delayed my growth. It's a bit funny now, remembering my shenanigans, at the same time, a little embarrassing. I am the granddaughter and daughter of prayer warriors, survivors, and God-fearing women. It would be a dishonor to not keep in mind that it is their shoulders on which I stand.

Bra-stuffing is a lifestyle. One I have embraced completely. God really does have a sense of humor but His judgment is sure. Choosing unhealthy activities to become healthy actually makes the vessel unhealthier, possibly unto death. For eighteen years, I have had the pleasure of being chosen to be diagnosed and battle with a disease called breast cancer—not once but twice. For eighteen years, I have been prayed for and with for strength to endure and unwavering faith in God. Between checkups, exams, multiple surgeries, medications, relinquishing my dignity, and at least fifteen trillion tears, I can now say I am healed!

I cannot tell you how grateful I am to God and those He placed in my path to walk this cobblestoned road with me. Through fear of death, fear of the unknown, fear of rejection, anxiety, unanswered questions, physical and emotional struggles, never did I give up on God. Countless miles were placed upon my feet due to walking day and night, praying to the one true God for peace. From reading scriptures out loud to plain old thanking him for His mercy, I was covered. There were many others who fought just as hard but God had another plan.

Life has an odd way of coming at you like a freight train with the combined force of a hurricane and tornado. If we are not prepared, it will hurt more than we can imagine and the cleanup is enormous, causing overwhelming sorrow. The anger, stress, and sadness of a diagnosis is scary and real. But relationship cancer is just as damaging. Honest communication with your family to include the children promotes tolerance and allows the relationships to be restored daily.

We hear the words "God will be with you always," and it sounds untrue when the words "You have cancer" are uttered but He is there. He knew before you did. Take solace in the fact that you were chosen. Hold fast to your faith without wavering. When you face challenges, ask God, "What is it you want me to learn from this?" He will show you in His time. Be humble because we don't control anything. He may be leading you to a special treasure. Continue being obedient and thank Him for the bad because the good is coming.

Undershirts are not for babies. They add a sense of security and protection from outside environmental influences that are unhealthy, just as God provides us with covering to block us from the pressures of the enemy. We are all in training for something. It may be things we can't understand or see in our future. It may even cause us to wonder what God is up to and push us to fill our lives with things that foster more questions than answers. As a believer, angels are always in your pockets so there's no need to feel that you must go the path alone.

To the best of my recollection, my Uncle David was the first man to offer me a lifeline without wanting anything in return. I remember when I was little, we lived two houses down from him. I was at his home, having Sunday dinner. My Aunt Sophie made pot roast, rice and gravy, macaroni and cheese, and cornbread. We had sweet tea to drink. Aunt Sophie also had some ribs on the table on this day. She was trying to get rid of the leftovers in the refrigerator. I had gotten down to my last bite and all of my bread was gone.

"You want this piece of bread? I didn't put my mouth on it," he asked me.

"Yes, sir!" I said and took it out of his hands.

My cousin and I laugh about that to this day. As far as I know, my uncle was raised in Peachtree, Alabama, and though he'd been in California for more years than I could count, he never lost his Southern accent nor his manners. He was my first father figure and after him came Pastor M. The two of them, together, were the pillars I needed in my life story. Both are now resting in heaven and I can only imagine their conversations about me. ☺

Presently I am a professional bra stuffer, heading into my thirteenth year of remission from my second diagnosis but still working on becoming an expert in loving who I am as I am. I strive to help others who have been diagnosed with any type of cancer. I do this by joining them at doctor appointments, listening to their stories, praying with them and for them, and modeling the healed life. I still feel a little pinch of nervousness when the time comes for my yearly checkups. I believe that's normal. Going through five years of taking Tamoxifen, twice daily, and having menopausal symptoms and still having a menstrual period, losing my hair, gaining weight, and mood swings all the while trying to get used to being a survivor nearly broke me. I was being convicted by God to do more than wear a T-shirt and bracelet with a pink ribbon and to share my story. It was causing a rift in my relationship with God. I was reminded of what God had done for me once again and I am still learning how to be a survivor. I'm not looking for excuses or apologies. God does God-sized things, and when you understand that, you retain that information and it gives you strength. People don't understand how

I have joy when I have undergone such traumatic experiences. Joy is an inner disposition of the soul.

God is constantly taking me through a transition. I have been made to stand out, stand up, and stand firm on the promises of God because He has a plan for me. I didn't lose a breast to cancer. God took away what was representing something unhealthy in my life. I promised God that from now on, He can use me for whatever He wills.

Lord I know I've made mistakes, I'm gonna do whatever it takes
Because I realize I need you in my life.
So I'm gonna turn around 'cause I'm Heaven bound
I'm tired of livin' with misery and strife.
So Lord, please show me what I need to do
All I want is to reconnect with you.

I broke your heart I made you cry as I watched the world go by
Not tryin' to reach those who needed you the most.
But Lord I know I'm ready now, with an humble heart I vow
To be a servant; to be a worthy host.
So Lord, please show me what I need to do
All I want is to reconnect with you.

I want you to use me. Use me for your service.
I want you to use me. Use me for your praise.
I want you to use me. Use me for your glory.
Lord, I'm ready now I know. Where you tell me I will go.

You can use me. Lord I know you can
Remember Paul was just an ordinary man.
You can use me starting with today
I'll be Your servant show me the way.

My story is still being written and the journey continues.

The picture Chuck E. Heaton colored for me

QUESTIONS FOR REFLECTION/ JOURNALING/NOTES

1. Have you been diagnosed with cancer of any sort? If so, what are your thoughts on the contents of this book?

   _____
   _____
   _____
   _____
   _____

2. What, if anything, was encouraging or helpful about this book?

   _____
   _____
   _____
   _____
   _____

3. What portion(s) do you most connect with?

   _____
   _____
   _____
   _____
   _____

4. Is there someone in your life that you can be more helpful to them on their journey?

_____
_____
_____
_____
_____

Websites to research are: www.acs.org and www.cancer.org.

For current survivors and fighters:

- Know your body.
- Early detection is the best protection.
- Age, race, gender, or religion does not matter to cancer.
- If you feel something, say something. Trust your instincts; *You're not alone.* Crying anywhere and anytime is allowed!
- It's okay to be scared.
- Track your process by journaling as often as you can. It is therapeutic.
- There are no dumb questions to ask your doctor.
- Asking for help is not a sign of weakness; it's a sign of wisdom.

For caregivers:

- There is such a thing as too many questions. Know when to ask.
- It's not about you.
- Take care of yourself so you can take care of them.
- Be patient with them and yourself. Don't become the patient.
- Never underestimate the ministry of your presence.
- Don't feel guilty for needing and wanting to take a break.

I Stuff My Bra... *So What?*

(Shoulders hunch)

ABOUT THE AUTHOR

Laura A. Franklin is a two-time breast-cancer survivor. Her exceptional faith and courage has been tried and tested on many occasions. She not only emerged as a strong survivor but she emerged victorious and is a walking testimony of God's goodness, grace, and healing power. Her undaunted faith in God, coupled with her resolve and tenacity, has proven to be powerful lessons for even the most seasoned believer. Today Laura continues to exemplify unwavering trust and faith in the Lord despite negative medical diagnosis and prognosis. Her light shines brightly through her own life commitment and dedication to serve and pour into others what she knows to be the absolute truth about God. Hers in an extraordinary journey.

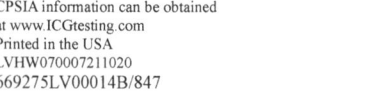

CPSIA information can be obtained
at www.ICGtesting.com
Printed in the USA
LVHW070007211020
669275LV00014B/847